.

Taking the Reins as CIO

"As a new CIO, I highly recommend this book to others taking on a similar role or on the CIO career journey."

—Naveen Krishna, EVP & CTO, *Macy's*

"When presented with your first opportunity to be a CIO, there are many aspects of the role you are ready for. There are many more that you are not. Acquiring these skills are like learning to swim in the deep end. This book helps to prepare the developing or inbound CIO for the unknown. Kudos to the authors for providing a long overdue book that delivers meaningful and usable knowledge for a very complex role."

—Rob Thomas, VP & CIO, *Kosmos Energy*

"The role of a CIO is complex, varied and volatile. Gerth and Peppard lay out a simple and easy-to-follow blueprint based on research from some of the world's leading CIOs."

—Justin Greis, Principal, *Advisory Services at EY*

"Tony Gerth and Joe Peppard have a unique understanding of the challenges that CIOs face today such as the art of balancing of relationships, cultivating a shared vision, raining in a constantly changing technology landscape, and understanding how to measure success. A great book for any CIO who is taking the reins for the first time or even been in the saddle for a while."

—Zach Vinduska, Vice President of Infrastructure, Security & Compliance, *ClubCorp*

"Kudos to Tony Gerth and Joe Peppard for such an informative and well-researched book of perspective, guidance, and frameworks that can propel CIOs to greater levels of success and influence in today's corporate environment. I would highly recommend *Taking the Reins as CIO* for all newly appointed CIOs who aspire to make a successful and lasting impact, and for other Senior Technology Executives who desire to move into the CIO role."

—Kim Batson, *The CIO Coach*

"*Taking the Reins as CIO* is a brilliant blend of pragmatic experience and academic rigor. It is rich with contemporary insight as digital demands grow and accelerate. I'll be recommending the book to both CIOs and the CxOs in many different disciplines who rely on digital technology for competitive success."

—Kevin Christ, Partner, *Concentre and Consulting Magazine* *Top 25 Consultant for Excellence in Technology*

"A rich, compelling, insightful analysis of how new CIOs can help organizations navigate digital transformation."
—Gianluca Carnabuci, Ingrid and Manfred Gentz Chair in Business and Society, and Associate Dean of Executive Education, *ESMT Berlin*

"When it comes to leadership best practices for CIOs there are loads of commentators that talk a good game, but Tony and Joe give CIOs a solid blueprint to make it happen. Basically a must read for every CIO or anyone who wants to become a CIO."
—Raj Ramachandran, Partner, *Heidrick Consulting*

"There might not be a more difficult role in organizations than CIO. Tony and Joe are experts on helping CIOs navigate the ambiguity and multiple land mines that come with their position and succeed. They have created a fantastic, much-needed resource for CIOs with this book, one that every CIO should read. It is so good that even seasoned CIOs will gain fresh insights and wish it had been available to them when they first started out."
—Andrew Neitlich, Director, *Center for Executive Coaching*

"This cutting-edge and innovative book on the novel but often misunderstood vital role of the CIO in 21st century organisation will be welcomed by both existing and aspiring future executives. It is written by two leading international experts in the area and unsurprisingly provides both the comprehensive and in-depth coverage necessary for a readership with serious intent in the CIO leadership space."
—Andrew Burke, Dean, *Trinity College Dublin*

"Tony Gerth and Joe Peppard cover important ground for any CIO, new or experienced in this unique book. The role of the CIO has never been under more pressure and is no longer limited to being a business leader and aligning technology strategy with business strategy. Instead, CIOs must be relevant to and in fact lead the digital transformations that are so key in today's business world as well as tomorrow's, as the Internet of Things will connect more devices than ever and take digital transformation for every company right to the 'edge'. This book builds on solid research and provides practical advice. A must read for any CIO leader on how to maximize their leadership impact!"
—Romil Bahl, CEO, *KORE*

"*Taking the Reins as CIO* is a great roadmap to success for a CIO, aspiring CIO or Executive leader looking to understand the role. With a great blend of research and practical application, this guides you to take charge and stand out."
—Sean Olson, CEO, Coach, Speaker, and Author, *This Is How I Role*

"As the lines continue to blur between new digital business models, process optimization, and enabling technologies, the role of the CIO is becoming more and more critical towards providing target customer and user experiences that allow companies to not only survive but get ahead in the market. *Taking the Reins as CIO* takes a research and evidence-based approach that offers insights and practical advice to both new and experienced CIOs alike.! must read for any CIO looking to play a leadership role in the successful growth and performance of their company."

—Eric Rich, Partner, *Elixirr*

"A timely and vital roadmap for how newly appointed CIOs can boost their success in today's digital world of myths and missteps. Packed with unique insights, this book is a must read for ALL C-suite executives (and Board members), whether new to their jobs, or in place for years. Gerth and Peppard's pragmatic leadership recommendations are a powerful, one-of-a-kind blend of (a) 10 years of inspired research, (b) analysis of hundreds of CxO conversations, (c) their own work experience as leaders in business, consulting and academia, (d) new frameworks and (e) clear explanations. Providing myriad "aha's" in every chapter, this book is a bold eye-opener for all senior leaders who seek more from their people, their technology and themselves."

—Jack Keen, Managing Director and Co-Founder,
The Value Selling and Realization Council

"Upon learning I was selected to lead the corporate IT function of our soon-to-be spun-off company (not a divestiture), I did a search of the current literature to better understand the array of tasks and measures of success for effective IT leaders. I found there are many good books that cover the landscape from purely tactical/technical considerations up to the strategic, non-technical subjects an effective CIO must become conversant in, but not many addressing the needs of newly minted IT leaders.

After reading an early manuscript of Tony and Joe's new book I found the perspectives they shared resonated strongly with me and my personal experience as a new IT leader, especially the paradoxes contained within the role. I think *Taking the Reins as CIO* brings a wealth of insights relevant to today's ever-changing IT landscape with sound guidance on how to increase the odds of achieving success as measured by our business partners. This book should be required reading for any new CIO as well as seasoned leaders looking for fresh insights in effectively delivering on the role."

—Bob Rosen, Vice President of Information Technology, *Arcosa, Inc.*

"Digital transformation is affecting the role of the CIO dramatically. If you're an aspiring or newly appointed CIO, this book is a must read! Written by two experts, the book shows in a highly practical way how CIOs can take charge and stay in charge throughout their career."

—Martin Mocker, Professor of Information Systems, *Reutlingen University and Research Affiliate of the MIT Sloan Center for Information Systems Research (CISR)*

"Whether you're a new CIO or have joined a new organization, *Taking the Reins* is full of research-based practical advice to help you succeed. Keep it close!"
—Blaize Horner Reich, RBC Professor of Technology
and Innovation, *Beedie School of Business*

"The fundamental problem with being the CIO is that the CIO-role seems fundamentally different from any other role in the IT department, and those that built their careers in IT basically arrive unprepared for this (great) job. Within a short timeframe, they must learn everything about businesses, markets, competition, manufacturing, finance, politics and the often pretty strict executive manners. Subsequently, they often have to align business turbulence and stovepipe legacy systems. For all those CIO's, Gerth and Peppard's book is compulsory reading. The book includes the latest thinking in IT governance frameworks and ample advice based on their rich experience with companies around the globe. The book is also valuable reading for the other members of the board, who may be interested in understanding the CIO challenges and the impact IT innovations could have in your organization. Basically, all managers are primarily managing digital innovations these days."
—Egon Berghout, Academic Director of IT Auditing
and Advisory, *Erasmus University*

"Using research and evidence, Tony Gerth and Joe Peppard created a strong reference guide for the newly-appointed CIO to forge a path for both initial and sustained success. I believe this book is also equally useful for aspiring CIOs and internally-promoted leaders. The historical context on the evolution of the CIO role is a insightful journey into the role confusion that plagues CIOs today. Understanding the authors' presentation of CxO frames of reference on the CIO role will also help newly-appointed CIOs craft the right influencing techniques and determine how to best build credibility early on so they can have the license to invest in innovation. When making those investments, the authors highlight the need to negotiate and track IT performance measures to define success as well as benefits realization. I appreciated the focus on typical personality profiles for IT leaders and how to overcome blockers to be successful. I also found the focused tips around operational performance, governance and team talent valuable. Overall, I strongly believe many points in this book will resonate with the reader from their own experience and will give them insights to the multi-dimensional complexities they will face in a new CIO role."
—Chris Catalano, CIO of HR Technology, *GE*

"This book is important to all members of an Executive Committee; it is filled with insights relevant to defining their and their newly appointed CIO's responsibilities for working more effectively together to create significantly more value from digital resources."
—Nils Fonstad, Research Scientist, *Center for Information
Systems Research, MIT Sloan School of Management*

Tony Gerth • Joe Peppard

Taking the Reins as CIO

A Blueprint for Leadership Transitions

palgrave
macmillan

Tony Gerth
North Richland Hills, TX, USA

Joe Peppard
MIT Sloan School of Management
Cambridge, MA, USA

ISBN 978-3-030-31952-6   ISBN 978-3-030-31953-3   (eBook)
https://doi.org/10.1007/978-3-030-31953-3

This Palgrave Macmillan imprint is published by the registered company Springer Nature Switzerland AG.
The registered company address is: Gewerbestrasse 11, 6330 Cham, Switzerland

Preface

The label of Chief Information Officer (CIO) has been around for nearly four decades, although the origins of the role itself actually date back to when computers first entered organizations. Yet, compared to other leadership positions, it is a deeply ambiguous role and not without its controversy. Poll any C-suite as to what the role entails, and you are likely to get as many perspectives as there are members. Responses are likely to be as varied as portraying it as a purely technical position, responsible for ensuring that the organization has the right systems to function and that they are resilient and cost effective to describing the CIO as being responsible for addressing the challenge of the disruption being brought about by technology and to drive innovation and digitally transform the organization.

Part of the problem is that, perhaps more than any other role in the C-suite, the CIO role has evolved significantly. What began very much as a technical role at the periphery of an organization and its activities has evolved to be concerned with something that is fundamental to not just how an organization works but increasingly core to its sustaining its competitive positioning or meeting its mission.

Today, few, if any, organizations could exist for very long without their IT systems. New digital technologies are challenging long held assumptions about everything from the nature of products and services and employee experiences to the very essence of organizations themselves. Many traditional industries are facing considerable disruption, while others are being eliminated altogether. Platform organizations are becoming increasingly dominant, powered by data, with their ecosystems fueling their growth. So while technology is very much center stage, many organizations are struggling to cope with this revolution that is coming at them at pace. "What should we do with

IT?" "How should we best manage IT?" "How can we best leverage the digital opportunity" or "How can we prevent being Ubered?" are just some of the questions that we often hear. What is becoming increasingly obvious is that this revolution hasn't always been matched by the required mindset shift across the C-suite to succeed in the digital economy.

More than any other role, the success of a CIO is heavily dependent on the active engagement and involvement of others—a challenge for a CIO is that their peers often do not see it that way. Perhaps this lack of understanding of the mechanisms through which technology impacts strategic and operational performance contributes to the challenges that many CIOs continue to face. To use a sporting analogy, as a CIO you may be the striker or wide-receiver on your soccer or football team, but if your teammates fail to get the ball to you, no matter how great a player you are, you can run up and down the pitch all day long but you will never score!

What we do know is that CIOs cannot accomplish business value objectives from technology in isolation from the rest of the business.[1] This points to a conundrum that some CIOs have long faced: being held accountable for achieving business outcomes without having control over the resources necessary to get things done.[2] With the current dominant models for IT in most organizations,[3] the CIO and his/her organization can only ever deploy and provision technology; galvanizing the rest of the organization around achieving the necessary change is usually a challenge. Investments in digital are less about investments in technology than they are about investments in change.

The paradox is that the IT unit—which the CIO heads—is expected to be a value-added contributor but often treated like a service provider. The constraints that such a view imposes see IT (both "the tech" and "the function") in many companies, unfortunately, having a poor reputation.[4] In some organizations, their IT unit must take some of the blame for contributing to this situation. Their lack of focus on the dynamics of the business, their sometime slow response to requests and strict adherence to plans and timelines mean that they are not known as the "Department of No" for nothing!

And, of course, we cannot forget about the legacy; the technical debt that has accumulated, often after years or even decades of underinvestment. Moreover, as organizations look to become more customer centric, they find that how systems were built in the past—around processes or products—pose significant challenges for them in their quest to place customers' center stage. All this only serves to create a virtuous negative cycle that contributes to a continually widening gap between IT and what is euphemistically known as *the business*.

Perhaps this complex historical context points to some reasons for the unusually high attrition rates of CIOs? Data suggests that these are higher than other functional areas. Moreover, the involuntary turnover rate is higher than other executives. Being a CIO is primarily a leadership role and we know that leadership transitions are not always easy. One study suggests that half of all leadership transitions fail within two years.[5] We personally know CIOs with stellar CVs, who could demonstrate significant accomplishment, some of whom were even feted by their peers with industry and magazine awards, yet did not make it past the one-year mark in a new assignment. We also have many stories about CIOs being sidelined in their organization's digital ambitions, replaced by a new kid on the block, the CDO (aka Chief Digital Officer). The direct cost of replacing a new leader is a multiple of many times their base salary. For a newly appointed CIO to integrate successfully into a new assignment and to be effective as soon as possible is crucial for both the executive taking on the role and the hiring organization.

Taking up a CIO role with all this as a backdrop is daunting. How should you approach the job? What are the first areas you should attend to? What do you look to accomplish over the first few weeks and months into the role? Are there any decisions that you can postpone making? What are the most important concerns to address? What are the "speed bumps" to look out for?

This book is for newly appointed CIOs and seeks to provide them with the guidance to take charge in their new role. Taking charge is essentially the process of learning and taking action that a newly appointed CIO goes through until he/she has mastered the new assignment in sufficient depth to be effective in the role.[6] Whether as a first appointment or the 21st, this is not a trivial process, but our research with those who have taken on the role reveals some common patterns and themes that have enabled us to present guidelines that will increase the likelihood of success.

The book will also be of interest to aspiring CIOs, those already in senior positions who are looking to make the next big leap in their careers. It will give them some pointers in relation to areas they should possibly seek to develop as well as areas to focus on during the recruitment process.

This book is not a book about leadership per se, although your leadership capability will also be part of what determines your success during the early months of your transition. There are many books and articles on the leadership topic. Even a cursory glance reveals that there is a myriad of views on what it takes to be a successful leader. We do know is that no one approach guarantees success; it is about tailoring your approach to the organization and its context.

A Golden Age for CIOs

This is the golden age for CIOs! Never has it been a better time to be a great CIO. Never has it been a worse time to be an average one! The focus that many organizations have on "becoming digital" has opened up tremendous opportunities for CIOs to take the reins and drive their organizations forward in leveraging the capabilities afforded by new technologies. This is more than successfully running IT projects, maintaining the resilience of IT services or modernizing the infrastructure. It is about leading the fundamental rewiring of an organization and its offerings.

Working across the enterprise, CIOs have an intimate knowledge of its structures, processes and information flows. They know the importance of integration while at the same time understand the consequences of standardization. They are immersed in data: data is at the forefront of their thinking. They understand how crucial resilience and security is and the need to protect digital assets. They think in systems, recognizing the interconnectedness of what might seem like discrete elements, and acknowledge the crucial role of architecture. Agile, which has recently found its way into the lexicon of mainstream business management, has long been a way of working in IT units. Most have worked with an ecosystem of IT service providers and technology vendors for many years. Crucially, CIOs know technology, and innovation is the central plank of the IT industry, an industry that is shaping the digital revolution.

The Research Underpinning This Book

The challenge of taking charge as a newly appointed CIO has fascinated both of us. The initial impetus came from research that one of us (Joe) undertook as part of the design of an IT Leadership program he was initiating while on the faculty at Cranfield School of Management in the UK. This executive education program, targeted at aspiring CIO, was seeking to help participants who would join the program accelerate their careers through the development of areas critical to be effective in an IT leadership role. The challenge of taking charge really came to the fore when graduates of the program took up their first appointments as CIOs and begun to ask for some guidance. On surveying the landscape there was surprisingly no research that had actually studied what CIOs should do in the early days, weeks and months of their tenure.

For Tony, the origin of his interest in the topic was the result of working with CIOs as a partner with a global management consulting firm, helping them in their role. Now as a coach and educator he finds himself working with organizations to help them on-board newly appointed CIOs as well as directly with CIOs as they navigate a new assignment.

With this dearth of research, we joined forces to study how CIOs become effective in the role. We spoke with CIOs, CxOs, consultants, analysts and headhunters to better understand the dynamics of taking charge. We wanted to capture the experience of CIOs in taking change, the mistakes they made, the lessons they learned and the advice they would give their peers. We also wanted to understand the perspectives of other business leaders in relation to CIOs they have worked with and their expectations for the role. Of particular interest was exploring with them when CIOs "derail", and what they believed were the key reasons and contributing factors.

Headhunters provided us with insights as to what boards of directors and recruitment committees are expecting from the CIOs they were seeking to hire. Consultants working with clients shared with us what they had observed as they engaged in assignments with client organizations.

Increasing our understanding of how CIOs take charge provides insights that will increase their probability of successfully taking charge of a new assignment. This does not merely refer to a first assignment but to taking up any new appointment as a CIO. What has emerged from our research is that the early days, weeks and months can set the tone for the newly appointed CIO. Of course, this is no different than for other leadership positions. However, we were interested in exploring as to whether there were any dominant pathways that would help CIO increase their likelihood of success; whether there are particular areas they should focus on. Are there any dos and don'ts during the early weeks and months of a new appointment?

All those that we spoke to had stories to tell, experiences to reveal and lessons to share. Our role as researchers was to search for patterns in what our interview data was revealing. As you work your way through the book, you will see the models and frameworks that we used to help us make sense of what we were being told. The prescriptions that we pulled out from our data were the result of us synthesizing the words of those we interviewed. In as much as possible we have tried to give voice to the words of our research collaborators; we use lots of quotes as these reflect scenarios and situations better than any words we could ever write. As you will see throughout the book, those we spoke to were very generous with their time and frank in answering our questions, and as we guaranteed confidentially we don't use any names or information that might lead to identify anybody who contributed to our research.

The research portfolio that we draw on for this book has one objective, to help CIOs thrive in their role. While a lot of research has been concerned with producing tools and frameworks to help IT leaders be effective in the day-to-day aspects of their role (e.g. building an IT strategy, defining the enterprise architecture, managing the IT investment portfolio, running IT projects and managing IT services), this book focuses on helping them when they take up an appointment as a CIO. This might be as a result of promotion from within an organization, perhaps moving from Head to Infrastructure or Service Delivery to becoming CIO. It can also be the result of a recruitment drive that sees a CIO being brought into the organization from the outside. While most newly appointed CIOs tend to come from organizations within the industry, this is not always the case. Apart from coming from other industries, newly appointed CIO can come from supplier organizations or consultancies. Indeed, it is not even necessary that they come with a technology background. Whatever their background, they all have one overarching objective: help their organizations optimize the opportunity from digital technologies.

In our quest to better understand the challenge of taking charge we have also been influenced by the work of others. In particular, the pioneering work of John Gabarro had a significant impact on our own thinking about the taking charge process.[7] Michael Watkins and his work on leadership transitions, particularly the first 90-days of a new assignment, has also shaped our thinking.[8] The research on the theme of new leader socialization has similarly influenced our work.[9] Our scholarly colleagues in the information systems discipline have also explored many aspects of the CIO role that has guided our research. Where we have drawn on this work in our writing, we acknowledge their immense contribution.

Outline of the Book

The book begins by first exploring the role of a CIO and what it entails. As has been noted, it has evolved over the decades and continuous to do so, resulting in a C-suite role that has become very ambiguous. Apart from tracing the origins of this ambiguity, this chapter surfaces the consequences this has for a newly appointed CIO. The chapter also explores the emergence of Chief Digital Officers and Chief Data Officers (confusingly both CDOs!) and what this means for the positioning of the CIO and the IT leadership role.

Chapter 2 focuses on the organizational environment within which the CIO operates. As a CIO takes charge, it is imperative that he/she has a clear understanding of the different factors that can impact his/her ability to succeed.

These can strongly influence what the CIO can and can't achieve and the speed at which they can initiate changes they might deem necessary to make. Many of these factors are outside the direct control of any CIO; however, they can be in a position to influence them.

Chapter 3 examines how new leaders "fit in" (or don't) to an organization. It introduces research that lays the foundation for what will be discussed in the remainder of the book, as it pertains specifically to CIOs. The first stream of research we discuss is role theory, which describes how a person's role in an organization is shaped. Senior executives have more influence in how their roles are defined than others working lower down in the organizational hierarchy, who must primarily accept the organization's expectations. Organizational socialization describes the process of actions taken by the organization to shape how individuals fit into it. This process tends to be one way; describing how the organization acts on individuals. Leader socialization, on the other hand, is a much more complex process of mutual adjustment. The new leader must learn "how things are done around here" in order to fit in. However, they also have influence over the organization and the potential to shape expectations of their role rather than merely "fitting in" to existing expectations. Key messages of relevance for an IT leader are deciphered and their implications outlined.

Every CIO steps into an existing organizational situation when they take on a new role. This inevitably shapes the type of transition they face and is an important context for the appointment. For example, they might be coming into an organization where technology is seen as a problem, with a history of failed IT investments and significant relationship issues between the IT department, that the CIO will now lead, and the rest of the organization. Chapter 4 discusses these different transition contexts and the consequences these have for the taking charge process. It also showcases some "CIO stories", short vignettes that describe the "taking charge" situations that some of our CIO contributors encountered.

Chapter 5 presents the taking charge process that we discerned having analyzed our data. The following chapter then describes the three phases of this process in detail; what we label Entry, Stabilization and Renewal.

Chapter 7 offers the CxO perspective of the CIO role, particularly their insights as to why, from their experience, CIOs derail. These are the views of peers that CIOs will have to work with to shape and accomplish their vision. The research is overwhelming in its findings that success with digital is very much a team sport; galvanizing the leadership team around a digital vision and the actions that will be necessary becomes paramount. But this is often easier said than done.

Chapter 8 presents a framework that provides guidance for the CIO in building peer relationships and exerting influence. From our data, we identified different categories of CxOs that CIOs are likely to encounter in their work. Understanding these and how to engage and interact with each type is important in successfully taking charge. In this chapter, we also introduce the concept of social capital, suggesting that this is really what the CIO is building in the early weeks and months of their tenure. It provides them with the resource to get things done.

Chapter 9 provides guidance to CIOs on how to be more effective and ultimately play the role of a business executive with special responsibility for information technology. To this end, we identify ten key prescriptions for CIOs when taking on a new appointment that will maximize the probability that they will be successful.

Chapter 10 concludes with some direct advice from CIOs to CIOs taking on a new assignment. This counsel comes from our interviews with CIOs and provides some very useful guidance, particularly around the pitfalls to avoid.

In each chapter, where we have drawn on the work of others, whether research or commentary, we note this. Occasionally, we also point to further material where those interested in digging deeper into an area can find additional writings. Details as how to source all of this material can be found in the endnotes at the end of each chapter.

North Richland Hills, TX, USA   Tony Gerth
Préverenges, Switzerland   Joe Peppard

Notes

1. J. Peppard and J. Thorp, 'What every business leader should know and do about digital', *Cutter Business Technology Journal*, Vol. 30, No. 1, 2017, pp. 6–13; S. Maklan, J. Peppard and P. Klaus, 'Show me the money: Improving our understanding of how organizations generate return from technology-led marketing change', *European Marketing Journal*, Vol. 49, Iss: 3/4, pp. 561–595; D. Marchand and J. Peppard, 'Why IT fumbles analytics', *Harvard Business Review*, January–February, 2013, pp. 104–112; C. Ashurst, N. Doherty and J. Peppard, 'Factors affecting the successful realization of benefits from systems development projects: Findings from three case studies', *Journal of Information Technology*, Vol. 27, 2012, pp. 1–16; S. Maklan, S. Knox and J. Peppard, 'Why CRM fails—and how to fix it', *MIT Sloan Management Review*, Vol. 52, No. 4, Summer, 2011, pp. 77–85; J. Peppard, J. Ward and

E. Daniels, 'Managing for the realization of business benefits from IT investments', *MIS Quarterly Executive*, Vol. 6, No. 1, 2007, pp. 1–11 and J. Peppard and J. Ward, 'Unlocking sustained business value from IT Investments', *California Management Review*, Vol. 48, No. 1, 2005, pp. 52–70.

2. See J. Peppard, 'The conundrum of IT management', *European Journal of Information Systems*, Vol. 16, 2007, pp. 336–345.

3. New organizing models are emerging. See J. Peppard, 'The metamorphosis of the IT unit', *MIT CISR Research Briefing*, Vol. XIX, No. 7, July 2019.

4. The problematic relationship between the IT organization and the rest of the business goes back many decades. See J. Ward and J. Peppard, 'Reconciling the IT/business relationship: A troubled marriage in need of guidance', *The Journal of Strategic Information Systems*, Vol. 5, No. 1, 1996, pp. 37–65; J. Coughlan, M. Lycett and R.D. Macredie, 'Understanding the business–IT relationship', *International Journal of Information Management*, Vol. 25, Issue 4, 2005, pp. 303–319; L. Willcoxson and R. Chatham, 'Progress in the IT/Business relationship: A longitudinal assessment', *Journal of Information Technology*, Vol. 19, 2004, pp. 71–80; B. van den Hooff and M. de Winter, 'Us and them: A social capital perspective on the relationship between the business and IT departments', *European Journal of Information Systems*, Vol. 20, Issue 3, 2011, pp. 255–266 and K. Zolper, D. Beimborn and T. Weitzel, 'The effect of social network structures at the business/IT interface on IT application change effectiveness', *Journal of Information Technology*, Vol. 29, 2014, pp. 148–169.

5. S. Keller and M. Meaney, 'Successfully transitioning to new leadership roles', *McKinsey & Company*, May 2018.

6. This term "taking charge" comes from the work of Harvard Business School Professor, John J. Gabarro. Gabarro defined taking charge as "the process of learning and taking action that a manager goes through until he/she has mastered a new assignment in sufficient depth to be running the organization as well as resources and constraints allow". See J.J. Gabarro, *The Dynamics of Taking Charge*, Harvard Business School Press, Boston, 1987.

7. J.J. Gabarro, *The Dynamics of Taking Charge*, Harvard Business School Press, Boston, 1987.

8. M. Watkins, *The First 90 Days: Proven Strategies for Getting Up to Speed Faster and Smarter*, Harvard Business School Press, 2013; M. Watkins, 'How managers become leaders', *Harvard Business Review*, June 2012, pp. 65–72 and D. Ciampa and M. Watkins, *Right from the Start: Taking Charge in a New Leadership Role*, Boston, MA: Harvard Business School Press, 1999.

9. For example, B.E. Ashforth, D.M. Sluss and A.M. Saks, 'Socialization tactics, proactive behavior, and newcomer learning: Integrating socialization models', *Journal of Vocational Behavior*, Vol. 70, pp. 447–462, 2007; T.N Bauer, T. Bodner, B. Erdogan, D.M. Truxillo and J.S. Tucker, 'Newcomer adjustment during organizational socialization: A meta-analytic review of antecedents,

outcomes, and methods', *Journal of Applied Psychology*, Vol. 92, No. 3, 2007, pp. 707–721; J.L. Denis, A. Langley, M. Pineault, 'Becoming a leader in a complex organization', *Journal of Management Studies*, Vol. 37, No. 8, 2000, pp. 1063–1099; D. Downey, T. March and A. Berkman, *Assimilating New Leaders: The Key to Executive Retention*, American Management Association, New York, 2001 and B. Groysberg, A.N. McClean and N. Nohria, 'Are leaders portable?' *Harvard Business Review*, October 2006, pp. 32–41.

Acknowledgments

This book is for CIOs. But it could not have been written without the many CIOs who generously spent time with us, freely sharing their insights and experiences and were very patient as we sometimes probed them to elaborate further on the already-detailed responses that they had provided to us. There are also many others; non-CIO executives, board members, recruiters, analysts and academics who graciously agreed to be interviewed and shared their stories with us. We would like to express our gratitude to each and every one; you provided the crucial raw material that we worked with. We hope that we have done justice to your voices.

There were also many CIOs who provided feedback at presentations and workshops that helped us in developing frameworks and honing our findings and narrative. Some of the materials presented in the book have previously appeared in articles and we are indebted to the many reviewers and editors who provided us with feedback. Finally, we would like to thank the CIOs who personally wrote words of advice for CIOs taking charge that we have included in Chap. 10.

Contents

List of Figures

List of Tables

1

The Ambiguity of the CIO Role

For the last half-century, the role of the Chief Information Officer (CIO) has received growing attention from researchers, analysts, consultants, recruiters and, occasionally, the media.[1] While much has been written about this role, an unambiguous description of what exactly *being* a CIO actually entails has yet to emerge. Indeed, what is apparent from all the words that have been written is that the role of the CIO is anything but clear! Go around the room of most C-suites inquiring as to the nature of the CIO role and you are likely to get as many different responses as there are people around the table.

The source of all this attention can probably be anchored in the perennial problems that most organizations experience with their technology invest-ments and the questionable return boards and leadership teams believe they are achieving from their, usually, not insignificant spend.[2] Generally, it is the CIO who is held responsible for any disappointments to do with technology. The current "digital transformation" push of many organizations has again propelled the CIO into the spotlight. The pace of technological change means that chief executive officers (CEOs) are typically looking to their CIO to make the connection between technology and the business mission and drive the digital agenda. Yet, all the evidence suggests that organizations are strug-gling to achieve their digital ambitions.[3]

Perhaps as a consequence, CIOs have been reported as having a shorter tenure compared to other CxO roles.[4] While some CIOs may not be a good fit for the requirements of their role, a central factor contributing to an orga-nization's lack of success from IT is often the confusion about what a CIO is expected to achieve and the gap between expectations assigned for the role and the realities of what is possible within the constraints imposed by the

© The Author(s) 2020
T. Gerth, J. Peppard, *Taking the Reins as CIO*,
https://doi.org/10.1007/978-3-030-31953-3_1

leadership team. This latter situation was summed up by one CIO who said to us that, among other things, he was also expected to walk on water! This confusion has only exacerbated with the emergence of the chief digital officer (CDO), where job specs for this position seem to encroach on what many would consider as falling into the remit of a CIO.

This ambiguity around the role has implications for anyone taking up a CIO job. One thing is certain though: it can lead to significant frustration, not just for the CIO but also for the rest of the C-suite. Understanding the origins of the CIO position can help in understanding where this ambiguity has come from and point to how its impact might be eliminated. Indeed, we have found that there are actually different types of CIO, shaped by the scope of the role and strategic and operational choices that are made for the incumbent. This points to the fact that there may not be a single role descriptor. For any CIO taking up an assignment, it is important to consider this as it can impact both performance in the role as they shape expectations and how the incumbent is ultimately assessed and, more importantly, what they can achieve.

The Evolution of the CIO Role

To begin to understand the ambiguity surrounding the CIO role, it is helpful to trace its origins and examine at how it has evolved since it first arrived in organizations. Like many C-suite roles, the CIO role has changed over the years. However, unlike other roles, the role today is unrecognizable from early incarnations. Perhaps no C-level position has undergone as many changes in expectations, approaches and philosophies during the past few decades as that of the CIO. And the turbulent forces shaping businesses in today's always-on, connected and global marketplace promise to accelerate this ongoing evolution.

William Synott is generally credited with coining the label "Chief Information Officer" at the 1980 Information Management Exposition and Conference. In his speech, Synott introduced this new role describing it as responsible for overseeing an organization's information systems. He predicted that "*[t]he manager of information systems in the 1980s has to be Superhuman—retaining his technology cape, but doffing the technical suit for a business suit and becoming one of the chief executives of the firm. The job of chief information officer (CIO)—equal in rank to chief executive and chief financial officer—does not exist today, but the CIO will identify, collect and manage information as a resource, set corporate information policy and affect all office and distributed systems.*" Although it did take a number of years to catch on, the role was given broad recognition in 1986 when popular business magazine *BusinessWeek*, a perennial barometer of US board room thinking, ran a story announcing the arrival of the CIO. This it did under the banner "Management's newest star: meet the chief information officer".[5]

The genesis of the CIO role can be traced to a shift from IT having a supporting role in organizations, automating previously manual back-office tasks, such as payroll, accounting and inventory management to being a source of innovation and competitive advantage, driving strategic change. This shift demanded considerably more than just a focus on specifying, deploying and operating IT, which was the role of the CIO's predecessors: computer managers, data processing managers, eDP managers[6] and IT Directors. The new role required business-driven approaches to exploiting information and the capabilities of technology. Increasingly, information was recognized—at least in some quarters—as a critical resource that required active management, stewardship and oversight from a senior management perspective.[7] Even Michael Porter, the doyen of strategy, got in on the act when he postulated how information could give organizations a competitive advantage.[8]

The newly created position of CIO emphasized information over technology, enterprise over function and strategy over operations. Incumbents were still responsible for technology, in so far as it provided a capability, but the role had expanded. In addition to the operational dimensions, the position had a key requirement to provoke executive-level discussions across the organization relating to how information and technology could be leveraged, particularly in the pursuit of competitive advantage.

Prior to the 1980s, the role could be described as a back-office, functional one. The precursor to the CIO was head of an organizational unit, responsible for delivering IT services and applications and maintaining the necessary computing infrastructure. As essentially a technical role, IT was seen as subservient to the business, and the job of the "CIO" reflected this. There were, of course, a few organizations that saw the potential for technology to be a source of competitive advantage and the CIOs of these organizations played a more strategic role. Companies such as Frito Lay, Otis Elevators, Baxter Healthcare, American Airlines, Fedex, Walmart and BP were among a small number that harnessed IT as a source of competitive differentiation.[9]

It was really only with the arrival of PCs in the 1980s that computers become affordable to even the smallest organization and became more mainstream. Supporting knowledge workers, office automation (OA) became an objective that accelerated when networking capabilities were available toward the end of that decade. In most cases, however, this new office technology merely replaced traditional paper-based applications: typing (i.e. word processing), financial calculations and modeling (i.e. spreadsheets), record keeping (i.e. data bases); and with the arrival of networking technologies, internal memos (i.e. email). Despite the increasing profile of IT, the CIO role was still seen primarily as a technical one.

If *BusinessWeek* announced the arrival of the CIO, it also speculated its demise. In response to the challenges that companies were facing with their technology investments at the time—a situation that still prevails to this day—it ran another story on the CIO role at the end of the decade. This time, it suggested that for many incumbents taking on the poisoned chalice of CIO often meant "Career Is Over".[10]

In the early 1990s, business process reengineering (BPR) raised the profile of technology and, in some organizations, the status of the CIO. This was also the beginnings of enterprise resource planning (ERP) systems implementations that are still with us today. Organizations were strongly advised not to "pave the cow path" when deploying technology but rather to look to the opportunities that technology provided to re-imagine processes and workflows.[11] While essentially an operational and efficiency play, because technology was relatively new at seeking this scale of integration at an enterprise level, companies could gain a competitive advantage by successfully rolling out technology.

However, companies had mixed results with their investments.[12] The failure of many reengineering initiatives was usually not because the technology didn't work (although there were, and still are, examples of this) but primarily due to the failure to successfully manage the associated organizational change.[13] As was noted by one commentator at the time, it was the "*fad that forgot people*",[14] a nod to the continual challenge that organizations have with their technology investments.

The CIO role gained added exposure from the mid-1990s with the internet opening up for commercial activity. Companies rushed to establish an online presence and build e-commerce channels, looking to their CIO to source and build the necessary technology. With new technologies, "knowledge management" entered the fray. This also coincided with efforts to address the year 2000 problem (Y2K), the so called millennium bug. That no major catastrophe resulted from the switch-over to the new millennium was due to the planning and execution of CIOs, although for some in C-suite, the CIO was seen as perhaps overplaying his/her hand. The role lost its luster a bit with the dotcom bust a few short years later. Indeed, the situation at the time led the ever-influential *Harvard Business Review* to run a contributed article titled "Are CIOs obsolete?"[15]

It was also at this juncture that IT outsourcing reached fever pitch. Ever since Kodak outsourced their IT systems in 1989, the first time a large global corporation had done so, it become a popular strategy.[16] For many organizations, IT was not seen by their leadership team as core to their main business and an obvious candidate to have performed by someone else. It had an added bonus of ridding the organization of what was perceived as a "problem". Over the years, outsourcing has tended to ebb and flow with business cycles: in down turns it is usually seen as an attractive proposition. But as we have seen in recent years, this has led to some companies, particularly in automotive, retail and energy industries, now grappling to rebuild this capability that is now core to competing in the digital economy.

The nail in the coffin for the CIO came in the form of Nicholas Carr's 2003 article "IT doesn't matter", published in the *Harvard Business Review*.[17] This article reinforced many of the prejudices that executives often hold in relation to technology. Carr argued that investment in IT, while profoundly important, is less and less likely to deliver a competitive edge to an individual company. "*No one would dispute that information technology has become the backbone of commerce*", Carr said, but "*The point is, however, that the technology's potential for differentiating one company from the pack—its strategic potential—inexorably diminishes as it becomes accessible and affordable to all.*" Because it was published in such an influential outlet, executives now had strong support in arguing the requirement for a strategic perspective was no longer necessary. The consequence was that in many organizations it setback the progress that had been made over many years.

Over the last decade, big data, analytics, mobile devices, internet of things (IoT), artificial intelligence (AI), blockchain and other technologies have again brought technology to the fore and witnessed the resurgence of the CIO. A slew of new entrants in the form of startups, the emergence of big platform companies and new digital business models have once more accelerated technology to the top of the agenda of most companies. No company wants to be "Ubered!" Software is well and truly "*eating the world*"[18] and digital transformation has become the new watchword. Add in cyber security threats, complying with General Data Protection Regulation (GDPR),[19] the game-changer implications of cloud computing and mobile personal devices, and the ingredients are all there to yet again to thrust the CIO role into the spotlight.

So, what's different today? While there have always been pioneering firms seeking out opportunities to harness the capabilities of technology for competitive purposes, it wasn't typical. Despite the promotion of IT as a source of competitive advantage, for many companies just successfully deploying technology to help them run their business more efficiently was sufficient. If the statistics are to be believed, most are still struggling to do this. Indeed, one scholar has noted that for many firms, gaining a competitive advantage from technology was often down to luck![20] Another revealed that most examples of companies gaining a competitive advantage from IT during the 1990s were "one hit wonders", with very few managing to innovate in any consistent way. It has only really been in the last decade that proactively seeking out competitive opportunities from technology has become more mainstream, even mandatory. This quest has been accelerated with smart mobile devices, providing the opportunity to engage directly with end customers, and the sheer volumes of data that organizations generate and have access to. Information and technology can no longer be ignored or relegated to the back-office.

Understanding the Causes of CIO Role Ambiguity

Over the decades, technology has become pervasive and businesses have become ever-more dependent on IT as technology and competitive differentiation become intertwined. As a consequence, CIO responsibilities have diversified to such an extent that differing organizations now have different authority profiles and positioning in the organization for their CIOs—at least for those whose job title is "CIO". CIOs have also assumed increasing responsibilities—sometimes reluctantly and with a realization that many of these responsibilities best lie outside of the IT organization, but in the absence of anyone else stepping up to the plate take on the responsibility.

Indeed, when you study the CIO role, what is interesting is that over the years it has accumulated more and more responsibilities. In the early days of computing, the job of the incumbent was effectively to make sure that the technology continued to function. Achieve this, and you were successful. Today, that may be an expectation, but it sits alongside being a strategic partner, an innovator, sourcing and driving the organization forward by harnessing the capabilities of technology, achieving the necessary change and driving revenue. Table 1.1 illustrates how the role, in general, has evolved through the different technology eras, with the shaded arrow showing the accumulation of responsibilities. This even led one scholar to question whether the role had become too big for one individual.[21]

Despite the opportunity that the increasing importance of technology provides for CIOs to raise their impact in the "C-suite", many have struggled. While some may not be up to the job, the lack of impact can be attributed to two aspects that are outside the direct control of the CIO. Firstly, the polarized

Table 1.1 The evolution of the focus and function of IT in organizations and the shifting role of CIO

	1950s	1980s	1990s	2010s
	Mainframe/early mini computer era	Distributed (PC, networking) era	Web-based, Internet and emerging mobility era	Smart computing, cloud and intelligence era
Major tasks of CIO	• Manage IT department • On-time delivery • Reliable IT operations	• Define portfolio of IT investments • Provide reliable and robust infrastructure • Office automation • Integrate the enterprise by aligning business and IT	• Knowledge management • Reengineer processes • Build e-commerce capability • Build alliances with key IT vendors • Ensure agility of IT platform • Lead innovation and change • "Right source" resources	• Re-wire organization for digital • Ensure integrity of IT supply • Secure and protect data • Conceive new sources of revenue from digital • Leverage data • Experimentation • Co-evolve with customers/ecosystem
Role of CIO	*Functional head* • Operational manager • Deliver on promises	*Relationship builder* • Strategic partner • Technology advisor • Align IT investments with business strategy	*Business leader* • Visionary • Innovator • Strategic thinker • Diplomat • Reading the market	*Orchestrator* • Lead digital agenda • Transform customer experience • Building business capabilities • Manage contracts, risk, security, privacy and service performance • Drive revenue

Source: Authors

views of CxOs about the role of technology in organizations.[22] Secondly, divergent perspectives for what it takes for success with technology, including where accountabilities should lie.

Regarding the former aspect, is the conviction at one end of the spectrum that IT is an administrative expense and a cost to be minimized. At the other end, there are CxOs who believe that information and IT are critical to how the business works, offers significant strategic opportunities and must be a key item on the agenda of senior executives. This fundamental dichotomy is at the heart of the different perceptions of the CIO's role, job description, reporting relationships and what he or she is expected to achieve. Moreover, it also determines the level of engagement and involvement of CxOs in what might historically have been considered as issues and decisions falling within the realm of the CIO.

Perhaps a reason as to why this might be so was offered by the CIO from a European content and consumer business, with over 300 titles and 200 websites and a turnover in excess of £1.5 billion ($2.4 billion) who told us: "*One of the main reasons why there are so few CIOs [as opposed to IT Directors] in the U.K. is simply that very few chief executives have met or are even aware of really good ones.*" He went on to explain that, in his experience, most CEOs that he has encountered have an outdated view of the CIO role that is inappropriate for today's business environment. A recruiter in a boutique CIO search company was blunt in her assessment "*Most leadership teams [that she has dealt with] do not know what good is!*"

Inappropriate Frame of Reference

Notwithstanding the above, we are finding it increasingly unusual to encounter a CxO who does not acknowledge the critical role of technology today. However, what we are seeing is that even in situations where CxOs subscribe to a more strategic view for IT they often do not understand what *their* role is and the wider responsibilities of "the business" in optimizing value from any technology spend. While this lack of understanding has been attributed to poor levels of "digital literacy" or "IT savvy",[23] we would characterize this as having an inappropriate frame of reference (FoR) in respect of what it takes to be successful with technology. This FoR influences many aspects, including beliefs about the role of the CIO, reporting lines, the nature of executive engagement with the CIO and how information and technology is led and managed.

An individual's FoR is a lens through which they view the world. It is a complex set of assumptions and attitudes that are used to filter perceptions and create meaning. We perceive what we consider to be reality through subconscious frames. Because we see perceptions as real, we believe others must also see them as we do. It is as if we are wearing rose-tinted spectacles and naturally believe that the world has a red hue, and consequently that others will see it likewise. A FoR influences not only how people see things but also the decisions they make. If the role of the CIO and what it takes for success with technology is seen in a particular way, it will influence choices and expectations, defining the sphere of possibilities and shaping ambitions.

Perhaps we shouldn't be, but we are continually surprised with how many executives do not fully understand how IT generates value and what their role is in this process. They happily defer to the CIO on what they see as being a "technology issue". This behavior is promoted by a FoR advocating that once the right technology is deployed on time, to budget and that it works, a project behind an investment has been a success. Merely deploying technology is insufficient to ensure delivery of any expected business outcomes. Ensuring the necessary organizational changes that will unlock benefits has been a perennial challenge as making those changes is not the CIO's or IT unit's responsibility. Unfortunately, this often leads to a conundrum for a CIO where they can be held accountable for IT investment success, yet don't have control over everything that is necessary to make it a success.[24]

Perhaps indicative of the leadership team's FoR is the reporting relationship of the CIO. While Synott advocated the CIO having a similar standing to the CEO and CFO, even today this prescription has failed to gain widespread traction. CIOs have tended to report into the finance function, both a legacy of the past (accounting as one of the first functions to be automated) and also a deliberate strategy to keep IT costs, perceived to be too high, under control, a nod no doubt to IT being seen as an administrative expense.[25] One CIO described his experiences to us of reporting to the CEO and then, when a new CEO came on board, the CFO:

> My first 5 years I reported direct to the CEO… He retired, and after that I ended up reporting to the CFO for the last 2 years [the CIO decided to move companies after that]. I saw a big difference in my ability to be effective…it was diminished when I reported to the CFO. At that point I no longer attended the monthly corporate executives' meetings. So I was not as versed in what their strategy was and even their tactics were 8 months down the road because they would be working on these plans. I would be briefed on it for 5 minutes in the staff meeting but it is not like experiencing it live with these guys for 3 days at a

time every single month. It made me less effective because I wouldn't know some of the details. I wouldn't know some of what the drivers and issues were because you just get summary information about it. So our IT team was less effective than they were when I was reporting directly to the CEO because I was hearing from the horse's mouth without the handoff between the CFO and the CEO.

Until a leadership team has an appropriate FoR, there will be a constant battle between CIOs and their CxO colleagues about what it takes for success with technology. One interviewee cautioned: "*Companies need to know how to use a CIO—what outputs they should expect, what contribution to the bottom line and so on. You can illustrate this problem quite clearly by thinking about a listed company doing an analyst or investor meeting. Generally speaking, the CEO will know how to direct questions to the CFO, the CMO and so on. But I don't think the same would be true with regard to the CIO—because I don't think enough CEOs really understand what the CIO contributes, in theory and in practice.*"

The Silent 'I' in CIO

It is ironic that despite there being no mention of technology in the CIO job title, it is technology that invariably gets the attention! Just ask any C-suite member as to what a CIO does, and technology will inevitably dominate the conversation from the outset. Information is relegated, at best, to the background. More often than not, it fails to register. From a historical perspective we can understand this; however, as we have shown earlier, the whole reason for introducing the CIO label was to emphasize the critical importance of information. Remember, Synott's original definition of a CIO: "*a senior executive responsible for establishing corporate information policy, standards and management control over all corporate information resources*".[26]

This is not to suggest that technology is not important; it absolutely is! But it is important in the sense that it provides the capability to work with and use information in different ways and for different purposes. The capabilities of technology all center around what it permits organizations to do with information: capture it, transmit it, store it, manipulate it and present it. How these capabilities are harnessed for both operational and strategic ends is only limited by human ingenuity. Innovation is simply being creative in exploring ways in which information might be used in different ways, for example, to engage in a different way with customers.

Performance data, what might be captured on a dashboard, is nothing more than presenting information. Customer experience is shaped by information. For example, your "Amazon.com experience" is all about how the company uses information: from search, to recommendations, to ease of purchase, to tracking of delivery. What is often called "insight" comes from new knowledge and understanding gleaned from data. Sometimes, the organization may already have this data, such as with customer transaction data, or it may be necessary to obtain from another source. Interactions with customers and ecosystem partners take place via information. Indeed, the value of a platform company is determined to a large extent by information and interactions.

As we saw earlier in the chapter, there was a time when technology capability was delivered from company-owned software, servers and data centers. With cloud computing, this is changing, and these capabilities can now be provisioned over the internet from a public cloud. This can mean that there will be no actually physical technology to manage. However, for any leadership team, the one thing that doesn't change is the need to figure out from the myriad of technologies and the capabilities they provide how they will be leveraged, both operationally and strategically. This is the essence of the digital strategy process and the CIO can play a pivotal role in leading this.

The CIO Stereotype

One critical barrier to being effective in a CIO role is the existence of a CIO stereotype. Just as we tend to stereotype politicians (can't be trusted), estate agents (cowboys) and academics (not living in the real world), we have noticed in our interactions with CxOs and board members that many hold a stereotypical view of a CIO. While CIOs also tell us this, there is empirical evidence to support this observation.[27]

In social psychology, a stereotype is an over-generalized belief about a particular category of people. Stereotypes are generally defined as cognitive structures that contain individuals' knowledge, beliefs and expectations about a particular social group.[28] Stereotypes are generalized because one assumes that the stereotype is true for each individual person in the category. While such generalizations may be useful when making quick decisions, they may be erroneous when applied to particular individuals. More specifically, they can encourage prejudices.

Such prejudices usually take the form of CIO peers having an impression of what he or she can and cannot do. Our discussions with CIOs strongly indicated that this can represent a significant barrier to their effectiveness. The CIO of a public sector organization described his experiences: "*The CIO is typically regarded as being a technical person and so only interested in technical matters and discussions and almost excluded from discussions around critical business issues.*" One aspect of the stereotype highlighted by the CIOs interviewed was that they are not considered "*to be business players*".

In one study, the stereotypical CIO was described by respondents as being "nerdy", "techy", "innovative", "geeky", "detail-oriented" and "task focused".[29] We have also found that they are seen as "introverted", although we do have evidence to suggest that this is likely (which we introduce in Chap. 2). Most also shy away from engaging in corporate politics, seeing it as nasty and not recognizing it as part and parcel of organizational life.[30]

Another study went beyond the largely anecdotally based evidence and used psychometric testing to investigate the personal and behavioral characteristics of IT managers and compare these with reported characteristics of business managers.[31] The results indicate significant differences related to issues of control and consequent leadership behavior and task/relationship orientation. It is speculated that IT managers with the personality characteristics identified in this study may tend to position IT in a service rather than a strategic role and experience greater difficulties in negotiating relationships with business colleagues.

What is interesting is that CIOs are perceived to have more in common with IT professionals than business leaders. This might seem obvious as most come from the ranks of IT professionals. It might explain why, even when a CIO is a member of the C-suite, they do not seem to be granted the same leadership authority as other C-suite members.[32] This has obvious implications for taking charge.

While many of those we spoke to agree that a newly appointed CIO coming to the position with a positive reputation can dent the stereotype image, they also agree that it is still a considerable barrier to overcome. The Head of Technology at a UK Retailer commented: "*Sometimes there is an image problem with IT—they [his business colleagues] don't understand where we're trying to get to. There are some stereotypes. … IT is good at telling the business what it can't do rather than saying well, we could do this or if we did it this way.*"

CIOs can also reinforce the stereotype and consequently their credibility. As the CIO of a global pharmaceutical company commented: "*If you have someone who is a geek [as a CIO], they will be put in the geek role and only expected to contribute to the narrow technical things like keeping the networks running, keeping the servers up, the operational stuff. Whereas if the person in the role is seen to understand the business and contribute to it, their role will be more highly valued at peer group level. If the IS manager is seen merely as a technician, that's how they'll be positioned in peoples' minds and won't be seen as really adding value to the business—just part of the support."*

Paradoxes Confusing the Role

We also find that there are paradoxes associated with the role that also contribute to the ambiguity.[33] A paradox is a statement that, despite apparently valid reasoning from true premises, leads to an apparently self-contradictory or logically unacceptable conclusion.

Examples of these paradoxes include all the right words being used during the hiring process, advocating for the new CIO to play a key strategic and innovative role. Yet, the reality for many CIOs is that they are forced to spend most of their time on operational issues. Cost has always been a watchword in managing IT, with CIOs seen as the steward of cost mitigation and containment; yet, at the same time, the CIO is also expected to build new capabilities that require investment. A key mandate is to be efficient and predictable; yet, at the same time IT is expected to be responsive and agile. The IT unit is seen as a service provider, with significant parts often outsourced; yet CIOs are expected to drive an innovation agenda.

These contradictory demands can make it difficult for CIOs to fulfill all the expectations for their role. They also set contradictory expectations and demands on a CIO that make it difficult for incumbents to satisfy what top management requires from technology, other than that it doesn't cause them any problems.

Muddying the Waters: The Emergence of the CDO Role

In more recent years we have seen the emergence of a new role in organizations, the CDO or Chief Digital Officer.[34] Yet, when we read job descriptions for this role, they sound very much like what we would expect a CIO to do. So here's the thing: we believe that this reflects the fact that some CIOs may not be up to the leadership component of the role. They might be very accomplished technically, maintaining efficient IT services and keeping costs under control. But in terms of driving the business forward with the use of IT, they are struggling. Perhaps this might be due to the stereotype or reporting relationships. Indeed, when the CDO role first appeared, one commentator noted that it "succinctly captures the future direction of the CIO role".[35] A partner in a consulting firm cynically described a CDO as *the CIO the CEO wished he had!*"

The CDO is seen to play in the place where the enterprise meets the customer, where revenue is generated and the mission accomplished. They're usually put in charge of shaping and implementing the organization's digital business strategy. This is where it starts to get confusing—companies distinguishing between digital and IT—with digital seen as any engagement via technology with customers and the wider ecosystem and innovation around new digital offerings, everything else being IT.

CIOs should be well positioned to meet the expectations of the CDO role, but only if they view their position as leading the broad use of digital technologies across the business. They need to continue to play a major role in managing the use of IT in the daily operations of the company, as well as in exploring ways of improving the IT infrastructure and all IT-based processes. But, they must also work closely with all other senior executives to help them design and build new digital offerings. In addition, as companies look to grow their businesses by developing cloud-based services, they will also play a major role in helping to identify and build these new IT-based business opportunities.

Our research would suggest that the CDO role is a transitory one, perhaps a stopgap to shore up a weakness that some CIOs might have in digital engagement with customers and embracing opportunities around new digital business models.[36] Indeed, given the focus that digital is receiving, a number of CIOs have added *Digital* (or the word has been added) to their job title, now becoming Chief Digital and Information Officer (CDIO).[37]

Differing CIO Role Definitions

Of course, a perfectly reasonable question to pose is *who* decides what the CIO role should look like and what it should entail? Perhaps it is inappropriate to expect a single, agreed upon, definition.[38] Logically, the role will be defined by what the specific business requirements are. If information is not central to the strategy of a business (although we find it hard to see how this might be the case), then the role of the CIO will be fundamentally different than a company where information and technology shape business models, customer value propositions and define the nature of engagement with customers.[39]

A senior telecom analyst noted to us: "*if you think about it, the role of the CIO is defined by the business of the company. What I mean is that a CIO for a low volume, high margin fashion house is going to be very different from the role of a CIO in a major telecoms operator.*" While this response might seem obvious, it is actually a strategic choice made by the leadership team as there is no reason why a fashion cannot compete using information. Ambiguity around the CIO role can therefore be explained by the realities of different role requirements and expectations for incumbents.

When we studied what CIOs were expected to do, we frequently found differences between the picture painted by academics, analysts and recruiters and the realities of the role that CIOs actually play in organizations. In short, what CIOs were expected to do varied. For example, someone might be hired, given the title CIO and mandated to overhaul the organizations operational backbone, replace aging legacy systems and shift processing loads to the cloud so as to improve efficiency and reduce the cost to serve the customer. For some, this may not be seen as a "true" CIO role. But who decides the criteria against which to make this assessment? If the incumbent fulfills the expectations for the job specification they are hired into, does it really matter what it is called? Of course, a counter argument could be made that the incumbent is not being utilized to the extent that they could.

A particular role definition likely signifies where current focus of the incumbent CIO lies and can change as the dynamics of the business also change. Roles that have been suggested include strategist (aligns business and IT strategies), catalyst (instigates innovation through transformational change), technologist (frame critical technology architectures that will deliver value in the future), innovator (identifies and develops opportunities to deploy new IT-enabled processes and products/services that give the organization a clear source of competitive differentiation over its rivals) and facilitator (ensuring information skills and capabilities pervade every part of the organization).[40]

Additionally, multinational and multi-business businesses can have multiple positions with the label CIO, but who have very different job requirements. A business unit (BU) or line-of-business CIO typically has responsibility for aligning the IT investment portfolio with the business unit's strategy. In some companies, it is more of a "relationship" role, with services delivered from a central IT function or from an external provider. A corporate CIO, on the other hand, can be responsible for seeking (IT) supply synergies across the corporation and defining corporate standards and policies to ensure consistency across the technology infrastructure of the group and, depending on the nature of the business, the process and application landscape.

A partner in one of the global management consultancy firms succinctly captured the challenge posed by a company having both BU and Group CIOs: "*the CIO role is often [defined] at group level with operational IT depart-*

ments at the operating company level. In these situations, it's quite often the case that the group CIO is somewhat powerless because budgets are controlled by the operating companies. Whilst the group function may set such things as strategic direction, sourcing policy and preferred supplier, it is often the case that operating companies [with their own CIOs] choose to do their own thing since they control the actual spend. In such situations there's often very little that the group CIO can do about it."

Where Next for the CIO Role?

Given that the history of the CIO role is shaped by constant evolution, where next? Thirty years ago the late Max Hopper, former CIO of American Airlines, wrote in *Harvard Business Review*: *"a company trumpeting the appointment of a new chief information officer will seem as anachronistic as a company today naming a new vice president for water and gas. People like me will have succeeded when we have worked ourselves out of our jobs. Only then will our organizations be capable of embracing the true promise of information technology."*

Indeed, there was a similar suggestion by a number of our interviewees that the CIO role may be a transitory one. That is, as technology becomes part of the fabric of an organization, there is some indication that the CIO role, as articulated today, may eventually become redundant. In this regard, a word of caution was expressed by the CEO of a European telecommunications company, who commented: *"maybe what companies should really be focusing on is not the creation of a CIO role, but the infusion of IT and information through every role, and every aspect of the business. ... And I think as time passes, senior managers will come under pressure to become more IT literate. I think we'll see IT elements find their way into a wide range of job descriptions and managers' targets and objectives. Companies will increasingly recognize that IT has to be an integrated part of many, if not all, senior management roles. It won't be acceptable to have a situation in which the CEO, CFO or any other manager does not understand the ins and outs of the company's IT systems and strategy. I think it's clear that digital capabilities are becoming more important for companies across almost all industries, and as a result, digital literacy—in the form of IT literacy—will become increasingly important for all business leaders."*

The essence of the implication of this was eloquently captured by the director of an investment bank when he said *"I think the notion of a CIO for an investment bank sounds somewhat absurd, in the sense that information is the beginning, middle and end of what an investment bank does, and therefore everyone is responsible for it."*

The CEO of a telecom company was even more forceful, *"Our view is that IT and information are too important to vest in a single individual—it makes far more sense to make sure that IT and information are integrated parts of every function within the business. Of course, we will still have an IT department. But the responsibilities that a CIO might normally have—above and beyond keeping IT systems working—are best handled by the members of the management team responsible for marketing, operations, finance and so on."*

In some organizations, the CIO title has already been eliminated and sub-sumed into a role with broader responsibilities. Singaporean Bank DBS has merged technology and operations, with the Head of Technology and Operations also responsible for innovation and customers.[41] In its quest to be more like a software company, Spanish bank BBVA similarly has eliminated the role of CIO and instead has a Director of Engineering & Organization who is responsible for technology, operations and product.[42]

Does this suggest that the role might "go back to the future", so to speak, and again become a technology focused role? Only time will tell. What is certain is that whatever happens it will only add to the ambiguity and con-tinue to present challenges for the taking charge process.

Implications of Role Ambiguity for the Newly Appointed CIO

The existence of ambiguity leads to uncertainty about the expectations, behav-iors and consequences associated with a particular role. Ambiguity in the CIO role arises when the norms for a specific position are vague, unclear and ill-defined. Specifically, incumbents have a need to know others' expectations of the rights, duties and responsibilities of the role, the behaviors that will lead to the fulfillment of these expectations, and the likely consequences of these role behaviors. Role ambiguity results when this information is non-existent or inadequately communicated. Role ambiguity may also be caused by organiza-tional factors (such as rapidly changing organizational structures, job feedback systems) and individual factors (such as information processing biases).

The consequences of role ambiguity can include tension, job dissatisfaction and turnover. Research indicates that role ambiguity is positively correlated with both anxiety and propensity to leave (the role) and negatively correlated with several factors such as organizational commitment, executive involve-ment and job satisfaction.[43] The former might perhaps contribute to the reported high turnover of CIOs.

We believe that this ambiguity is a key reason why many organizations continue to struggle with their IT investments and in achieving their digital transformation ambitions. The implication of CIO role ambiguity is that strategic and operational opportunities from IT can be missed and any investments made in technology underperform. At worst, this ambiguity can place the very existence of the organization in jeopardy.

Most of the CIOs that we have spoken to over the years do have clear ideas about what their roles should encompass, what their contribution can be and what is required for success with technology. Where this corresponds with the expectations and understanding of their CEO and CxO colleagues, there is role alignment. The frustration for CIOs occurs when ambiguity in the role results in misalignment between their expectations of how they can contribute and the expectations for the role their colleagues have. Ultimately, generating business value from information and technology is a shared responsibility; it cannot be delegated solely to the CIO. What we are also seeing today is CIOs taking on responsibilities for not just technology but operations and sometimes even product, particularly where a digital product is concerned.

What all this suggests is that being a CIO won't be an easy ride, that's for sure! The ambiguity surrounding the CIO role has led one academic team to conclude: "*The CIO role is a unique executive challenge.*"[44] It is vitally important to have a clear picture of expectations. All colleagues may not hold a similar perspective about the role as you do. One CIO lamented "*you can go in an organization in a C-suite role, and your peers get what you do and your role is accepted and understood. In the CIO's case it's often times not the case. I mean, everybody kind of gets what the VP of Marketing and the VP of Sales and the VP of Manufacturing do. This comes back to the role understanding question that I've talked about and never really fixed.*"

As part of the due diligence before accepting a role, it is probably worthwhile to talk to future colleagues to get a sense of their view of technology and information and how both should be managed. The reality is that on taking up the CIO role, the CIO may need to work with leadership team colleagues to re-orient their FoR. If nothing else, it can give an indication of the challenges likely to be encountered.

Despite the ambiguity, there is increasing acceptance that being a CIO is a business leadership position on par with other chief officer positions as Synott recommended all those decades ago. The question often becomes whether the incumbent sees themselves as a leader of a functional area, that is, IT or a business leader of similar standing to other C-suite members. Unfortunately, we still encountered CIOs that fall into the former category.

Notes

1. In fact, studies exploring the nature of the CIO role have a long history. Seminal studies include B. Ives and M. Olson, 'Manager or technician? The nature of the information systems job', *MIS Quarterly*, Vol. 5, No. 4, 1981, pp. 49–63; R.I. Benjamin, C. Dickson and J. Rockart, 'Changing role of the corporate information systems officer', *MIS Quarterly*, Vol. 9, No 3, 1985, pp. 177–188; J.L. Donovan, 'Beyond chief information officer to network manager', *Harvard Business Review*, May–June 1988, pp. 134–140; J.C. Emery, 'What role for the CIO', *MIS Quarterly*, Vol. 5, No. 2, 1991, pp. vii–ix; C. Coulson-Thomas, 'Directors and IT, and IT directors', *European Journal of Information Systems*, Vol. 1, No. 1, 1991, pp. 45–53; C. Stephens, W. Ledbetter, A. Mitra and F. Ford, 'Executive or functional manager? The nature of the CIOs job', *MIS Quarterly*, Vol. 16, No. 4, 1992, pp. 449–467; L. Applegate and J. Elam, 'New information systems leaders: A changing role in a changing world', *MIS Quarterly*, Vol. 16, No. 4, 1992, pp. 469–490; M.J. Earl and D.F. Feeny, 'Is your CIO adding value?', *Sloan Management Review*, Spring, 1994, pp. 11–20; Y. Li, C.-H. Tan, H.H. Teo and B.C. Tan, 'Innovative usage of information technology in Singapore organizations: Do CIO characteristics make a difference?' *IEEE Transactions on Engineering Management*, Vo. 53, No. 2, 2006, pp. 177–190; D. Smaltz, V. Sambamurthy and R. Agarwal, 'The antecedents of CIO role effectiveness in organizations: An empirical study in the healthcare sector', *IEEE Transactions on Engineering Management*, Vol. 53, 2006, pp. 207–222; D. Preston, D. Chen and D. Leidner, 'Examining the antecedents and consequences of CIO strategic decision-making authority: An empirical study', *Decision Sciences*, Vol. 39, 2008, 605–642; D.S. Preston, D. Leidner and D. Chen, 'CIO leadership profiles: Implications of matching CIO authority and leadership capability on IT impact', *MIS Quarterly Executive*, Vol. 7, No. 2, 2008, pp. 57–69; M. Chun and J. Mooney, 'CIO roles and responsibilities: Twenty-five years of evolution and change', *Information & Management*, Vol. 46, 2009, pp. 323–334; J. Peppard, 'Unlocking the performance of the chief information officer (CIO)', *California Management Review*, Vol. 52, No. 4, 2010, pp. 73–99; J. Peppard, C. Edwards and R. Lambert, 'Clarifying the ambiguous role of the CIO, *MIS Quarterly Executive*, Vol. 10, No. 1, 2011, pp. 197–201; J.L. King, 'CIO: Concept is over', *Journal of Information Technology*, Vol. 26, 2011, pp. 129–138 and P. Weill and S.L. Woerner, 'The future of the CIO in a digital economy', *MIS Quarterly Executive*, Vol. 12, No. 2, 2013, pp. 65–75.

2. The failure rate for IT projects has remained remarkably high over the decades. For some recent failures, see UK Government's report into the failure of the Disclosure and Barring Service (DBS) and the Home Office to modernize the services the DBS provides to the public and employers, *House of Commons*

Committee of Public Accounts, Disclosure and Barring Service: Progress Review, Published on May 1, 2019. F. Kolf and C. Kerkmann, 'Lidl software disaster another example of Germany's digital failure', *Handelsblatt*, July 30, 2017, https://www.handelsblatt.com/today/companies/programmed-for-disaster-lidl-software-disaster-another-example-of-germanys-digital-failure/23582902.html; for some examples from Australia, see M. Ludlow, 'IT disasters now part of modern life', *Financial Review*, December 21, 2016, https://www.afr.com/technology/it-disasters-now-part-of-modern-life-20160628-gptyw6 and J. Sweeney and D. Korber, *Crash Course: Failure to Heed Early Warnings, Troubles of the Past Contributed to Payroll System Collapse*, A Report Prepared for Senate Budget and Fiscal Review Subcommittee No. 4, California Senate Office of Oversight and Outcomes, August 12, 2013.

3. For data on success rates of digital transformation see J.-F. Martin, *Unlocking Success in Digital Transformation*, McKinsey & Company, October 2018; B. Rogers, 'Why 84% of companies fail at digital transformation', Forbes, January 7, 2017, https://www.forbes.com/sites/brucerogers/2016/01/07/why-84-of-companies-fail-at-digital-transformation/#352e65d397bd and J. Macaulay, 'Most digital transformation fail, here's how to change', *CEO World Magazine*, March 30, 2019, https://ceoworld.biz/2019/03/30/most-digital-transformations-fail-heres-how-to-change-that/

4. See S. Rosenbush, 'CIOs, facing rapid change, tend to be younger, with shorter tenure', *The Wall Street Journal*, February 14, 2017 https://blogs.wsj.com/cio/2017/02/14/cios-facing-rapid-change-tend-to-be-younger-with-shorter-tenure/ and 'CIO stats: Length of CIO tenure varies by industry', *The Wall Street Journal*, February 15, 2017, available at https://blogs.wsj.com/cio/2017/02/15/cio-stats-length-of-cio-tenure-varies-by-industry

5. G. Bock, K. Carpenter and J.E. Davis, 'Management's newest star: Meet the chief information officer', *Business Week*, 2968, October 1986, pp. 160–172. It should be pointed out that as early as 1984, there was a suggestion that one-third of US corporations had a CIO role, if not in title. See Diebold Research Group, *Chief Information Officer Concept*, DRG, New York, 1984. Fast forward to June 2010, and *Fortune* magazine, another barometer of C-suite thinking, ran a story 'Tech executives stop cutting and get strategic'. This article posed the question *"with the economy growing, CEOs want chief information officers to help with marketing and sales, are the techies ready to step up?"* One year later, *Fortune* ran another piece "Technology chiefs belong in the C-suite", this time pointing out that CIOs are not just tech buyers but strategic thinkers.

6. Electronic Data Processing.

7. Applegate and Elam suggest that the rise of the CIO marked the transition from the data processing era to the information era. See L. Applegate and J. Elam, 'New information systems leaders: A changing role in a changing world', *MIS Quarterly*, Vol. 16, No. 4, 1992, pp. 469–490.

8. M.E. Porter and V. Miller, 'How information gives you a competitive advantage', *Harvard Business Review*, July–August 1985, pp. 149–160. See also F. Warren McFarlan, 'Information technology changes the way you compete', *Harvard Business Review*, May–June 1984, p. 98.

9. See L.M. Applegate, 'Frito-Lay, Inc.: A Strategic Transition (A) (Updated)', *Harvard Business School Case 193–129*, February 1993 (revised March 1993). F.W. McFarlan and Donna B. Stoddard, 'OTISLINE (A)', *Harvard Business School Case 186–304*, June 1986 (revised July 1990). B. Konsynski and M.R. Vitale, 'Baxter Healthcare Corp.: ASAP Express', *Harvard Business School Case 188–080*, February 1988 (revised February 1991) and M. Hopper, 'Rattling SABRE—New ways to compete on information', *Harvard Business Review*, May–June 1990.

10. J. Rothfeder, and L. Driscoll, 'CIO is starting to stand for Career Is Over', *Business Week,* February 26, 1990.

11. M. Hammer, 'Reengineering work: Don't automate, obliterate', *Harvard Business Review*, July–August 1990, pp. 104–112.

12. Back in the 1980s economist Robert Solow wrote about the so-called productivity paradox *"you can see the computer age everywhere but in the productivity statistics"*. R. Solow, 'We'd better watch out', *New York Times Book Review*, July 12, 1987, p. 36. There is a long history of IT investments underachieving or failing outright. See P.A. Strassman, *The Squandered Computer: Evaluating the Business Alignment of Information Technology*, The Economics Press, New Canaan, Connecticut, 1997 and *Information Productivity: Accessing the Information Management Costs of US Industrial Companies*, The Economics Press, New Canaan, Connecticut, 1997. See also A. Von Nievelt, 'Managing with IT: A decade of wasted money?' *Information Strategy: The Executive's Journal*, Vol. 9, No. 4, 1993, pp. 5–17; *Productivity in the United States, 1995–2000*, McKinsey Global Institute, October 2001; Butler Group, 'IT spending and profits are unrelated', *Butler Concept Report on The Economics of Information,* London, July 2001 and Standish Group work on IT project management at www.Standishgroup.com

13. C. Tiernan and J. Peppard, 'Information technology: Of value or a vulture?' *European Management Journal*, Vol. 22, No. 6, 2004, pp. 609–623; C. Sauer, 'Deciding the future for IS failure: Not they choice you might think', in W. Currie and R.D. Galliers, eds., *Rethinking MIS*, Oxford University Press, Oxford, 1997; C. Clegg, C. Axtell, L. Damadoran, B. Farbey, R. Hull, R. Lloyd-Jones, J. Nicholls, R. Sell and C. Tomlinson, 'Information technology: A study of performance and the role of human and organizational factors', *Ergonomics*, Vol. 40, No. 9, pp. 851–871; *The Challenges of Complex IT Projects*, The Royal Academy of Engineering, London, 2003 and C. Sauer and C. Cuthbertson, *The State of IT Project Management in the UK*, Templeton College, University of Oxford, November 2003.

14. T. Davenport, 'The fad that forgot people', *Fast Company*, November 1995. https://www.fastcompany.com/26310/fad-forgot-people

15. Commentary by D. Lapore, J. Rockart, M.J. Earl, T. Thomas, P. McAteer and J. Elton, in R.F. Maruca, 'Are CIOs obsolete?', *Harvard Business Review*, March–April 2000, pp. 56–63.

16. L.M. Applegate, 'Eastman Kodak Co.: Managing information systems through strategic alliances', *Harvard Business School Case 192–030*, July 1991 (revised September 1995). See also L. Loh and N. Venkatraman, 'Diffusion of information technology outsourcing: Influence sources and the Kodak effect', *Information Systems Research*, Vol. 3, No. 4, 1992, pp. 334–358 and R. Plant, 'A Kodak moment to reconsider the value of IT', *Harvard Business Review*, October 12, 2011.

17. N. Carr, 'IT doesn't matter', *Harvard Business Review*, May 2003, pp. 5–12. Carr later went on to predict the end of corporate computing. See N. Carr, 'The end of corporate computing', *MIT Sloan Management Review*, 46, 3, 2005, pp. 67–73.

18. In August 2011, Marc Andreessen wrote an article in *The Wall Street Journal* titled 'Why software is eating the world' that generated considerable attention. Andreessen wrote *"My own theory is that we are in the middle of a dramatic and broad technological and economic shift in which software companies are poised to take over large swathes of the economy. More and more major businesses and industries are being run on software and delivered as online services— from movies to agriculture to national defense. Many of the winners are Silicon Valley-style entrepreneurial technology companies that are invading and overturning established industry structures. Over the next 10 years, I expect many more industries to be disrupted by software, with new world-beating Silicon Valley companies doing the disruption in more cases than not."*

19. The General Data Protection Regulation 2016/679 is a regulation in EU law on data protection and privacy for all individual citizens of the European Union and the European Economic Area. It also addresses the transfer of personal data outside the EU and EEA areas. See https://ec.europa.eu/info/law/law-topic/data-protection/reform_en?

20. C. Ciborra, 'The grassroots of IT and strategy', in C. Ciborra and T. Jelessi, eds, *Strategic Information Systems: A European Perspective*, John Wiley & Sons, Chichester, UK, 1994, 3–24.

21. Michael Earl in R.F. Maruca, 'Are CIOs obsolete?', *Harvard Business Review*, March–April, 2000.

22. See M.L. Kaarst-Brown, 'Understanding an organization's view of the CIO: The role of assumptions about IT', *MIS Quarterly Executive*, Vol. 4, No. 2, 2005, pp. 287–301.

23. For a fuller discussion of this topic see J. Peppard, 'Unlocking the performance of the chief information officer (CIO)', *California Management Review*, Vol. 52, No. 4, 2010, pp. 73–99.

24. J. Peppard, 'The conundrum of IT management', *European Journal of Information Systems*, Vol. 16, Issue 4, 2007, pp. 336–345.

25. For study of CIO reporting structure and organizational performance, see R. Banker, N. Hu, P. Pavlou and J. Luftman, 'CIO reporting structure, strategic positioning, and firm performance', *MIS Quarterly*, Vol. 35, No. 2, 2011, pp. 487–504.

26. W.R. Synott, and W.H. Gruber, *Information Resource Management*, John Wiley & Sons, 1981, p. 66.

27. P.A. Gonzalez, L. Ashworth and J. McKeen, 'The CIO stereotype: Content, bias, and impact', *Journal of Strategic Information Systems*, Vol. 28, 2019, pp. 83–99 and L. Willcoxson and R. Chatham, 'Testing the accuracy of the IT stereotype: Profiling IT managers' personality and behavioral characteristics', *Information & Management*, Vol. 43, 2006, pp. 697–705.

28. Z. Kunda, *Social Cognition: Making Sense of People*, MIT Press, Cambridge, MA, 1999.

29. P.A. Gonzalez, L. Ashworth and J. McKeen, 'The CIO stereotype: Content, bias, and impact', *Journal of Strategic Information Systems*, Vol. 28, 2019, pp. 83–99.

30. For more on the topic of organizational politics for IT executives see K. Patching and R. Chatham, *Corporate Politics for IT Managers: How to Get Streetwise*, Butterworth-Heinemann, 2000.

31. L. Willcoxson and R. Chatham, 'Testing the accuracy of the IT stereotype: Profiling IT managers' personality and behavioral characteristics', *Information & Management*, Vol. 43, 2006, pp. 697–705.

32. D.Q. Chen, D.S. Preston and W. Xia, 'Antecedents and effects of CIO supply-side and demand-side leadership: A staged maturity model', *Journal of Management Information Systems*, Vol. 27, pp. 231–272 and M.L. Kaarst-Brown, 'Understanding an organization's view of the CIO: The role of assumptions about IT', *MIS Quarterly Executive*, Vol. 4, pp. 287–301.

33. M. Heller, *The CIO Paradox: Battling the Contradictions of IT Leadership*, Bibliomotion, Brookline, MA, 2012.

34. Confusingly, CDO also signifies chief data officer.

35. Irving Wladawsky-Berger, 'Why CIOs may morph into the chief digital officer', *Wall Street Journal Blogs*, November 18, 2012. https://blogs.wsj.com/cio/2012/11/18/why-cios-may-morph-into-the-chief-digital-officer/

36. This also seems to be the picture we are seeing from the Harvey Nash/KPMG CIO Survey, 2019.

37. Harvey Nash/KPMG CIO Survey, 2019.

38. For an early study of CIO roles, see V. Grover, S.R. Jeong, W. Kettinger and C.C. Lee, 'The chief information officer: A study of managerial roles', *Journal of Management Information Systems*, Vol. 10, No. 2, 1993, pp. 107–130.

39. J. Peppard, C. Edwards and R. Lambert, 'Clarifying the ambiguous role of the CIO', *MIS Quarterly Executive*, Vol. 10, No. 1, 2011, pp. 197–201. See also Y. Gong, M. Janssen, V. Weerakkody, 'Current and expected roles and capabilities of CIOs for the innovation and adoption of new technology', *Proceedings of the 20th Annual International Conference on Digital Government Research*, Dubai, United Arab Emirates—June 18–20, 2019, pp. 462–467.

40. For a thorough review of CIO roles see A. Hutter and R. Riedl, *Chief Information Officer Role Effectiveness: Literature Review and Implications for Research and Practice*, Springer, Cham, Switzerland, 2017. See also J. Peppard, C. Edwards and R. Lambert, 'Clarifying the ambiguous role of the CIO', *MIS Quarterly Executive*, Vol. 10, No. 1, 2011, pp. 197–201; D. Smaltz, V. Sambamurthy and R. Agarwal, 'The antecedents of CIO role effectiveness in organizations: An empirical study in the healthcare sector', *IEEE Transactions on Engineering Management*, Vol. 53, 2006, pp. 207–222 and M. Carter, V. Grover and J.B. Thatcher, 'The emerging CIO role of business technology strategist', *MIS Quarterly Executive*, Vol. 10, No. 1, 2011, pp. 19–29.

41. See S. Kien, C. Soh, P. Weil and Y. Chong, *Rewiring the Enterprise for Digital Innovation: The Case of DBS Bank*, Nanyang Business School, Publication Number ABCC-2015-004.

42. https://www.bbva.com/en/biography/ricardo-forcano/

43. T.C. Tubre, and J.M. Collins, 'Jackson and Schuler (1985) revisited: A meta-analysis of the relationships between role ambiguity, role conflict, and job performance', *Journal of Management*, Vol. 26, No. 1, 2000, pp. 155–169.

44. E. Karahanna and R. Watson, 'Information systems leadership', *IEEE Transactions on Engineering Management*, Vol. 53, 2006, pp. 171–176.

2

No CIO Is an Island

One observation puzzled us and led to a research initiative which forms the kernel of this chapter. We had seen CIOs who were seemingly doing an excellent job, some of what they had achieved was highly visible and received the plaudits of their peers. Then, often to great fanfare, they were recruited by another organization but within six months had moved on. They were still the same person, albeit with more experience than when they begun their previous job, yet they had somehow "failed". Why was this?

CIOs don't work in a vacuum. They have colleagues, who themselves have personal goals and agendas and, as we saw in the previous chapter, will have their own expectations for the incoming CIO. Organizational contexts are also different: structures and operating models differ; leadership teams and their dynamics differ; personalities across the C-suite differ and organizational cultures differ. Add in the ambiguous nature of the CIO role, and we have a complex landscape that poses a challenge for any new executive to navigate.

A lot of emphasis is placed by a hiring organization on ensuring that they get the "right" person for the role: that the person has the appropriate level of requisite competencies and experience and that they are a good "fit" with what the organization is looking to achieve with technology. Yet, what the data indicates is that *the organizational environment within which the CIO operates* plays a central role in the success, not just of the CIO, but also with the organization in leveraging the opportunities from information and technology. Indeed, our data reveals that there is no direct link between "the perfect" CIO (if such a person even exists) and the contribution of technology to organizational performance. Thus, just hiring a CIO who has all the vital competencies and experiences does not guarantee that they will be as effective

© The Author(s) 2020
T. Gerth, J. Peppard, *Taking the Reins as CIO*,
https://doi.org/10.1007/978-3-030-31953-3_2

in their new environment. In fact, getting the "right" CIO may be a necessary but not a sufficient condition. For the newly appointed CIO, understanding the factors that will impact performance is important in shaping the taking charge process.

The CIO's Theater of Operations

From our interviews we have constructed a model positioning the CIO's role and its relationship with business and technology outcomes. Analyzing our data reveals the factors that impact the effectiveness of the incumbent CIO; or more pertinently, the ability of the organization to optimize the value it generates from investments in information and technology. Figure 2.1 illustrates this model, highlighting these factors and the relationships between them. What the model signals is that there is no direct correlation between the CIO and organizational performance enabled and shaped by information and technology. This relationship is mediated by other factors.

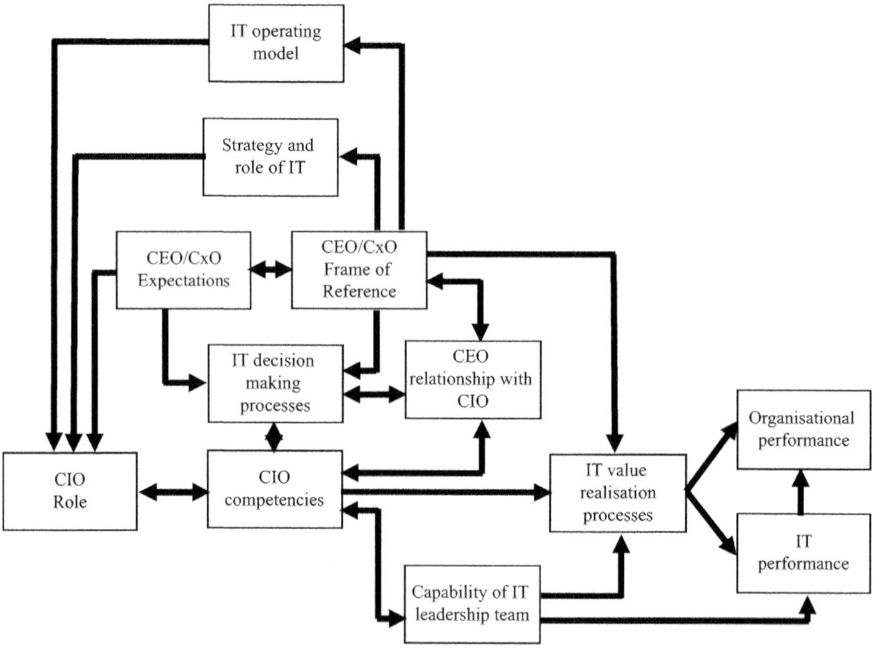

Fig. 2.1 A model linking the CIO role with organizational performance enabled and shaped by IT. (Source: Based on J. Peppard, 'Unlocking the performance of the Chief Information Officer (CIO)', *California Management Review*, Vol. 52, No. 4, pp. 73–99)

The Frame of Reference of the CxO Team

The one factor which stood out from all the interview data was the critical importance of the frame of reference (FoR) that the senior leadership team has for what it takes for success with information and technology. In the previous chapter we noted that this FoR shapes expectations for the role. But it also determines the CIO's relationship with the CEO and other c-level executives, the role that technology plays in the strategy of the organization, the design of the IT operating model, the effectiveness of IT and decision-making processes, all which ultimately determine whether the CIO will be successful in achieving business outcomes.

Although no one we spoke to directly used this term frame of reference, we have interpreted what they told us using this concept. Phrases like "IT savvy", "IT fluency", "digital literacy" and "IT literacy" were frequently heard during interviews. For example, a Director at a Global Investment Bank noted: *"I think an enabler [of a CIO's ability to deliver against expectations] is the level of IT literacy of the rest of the management team. The more the management team understands IT and what is required for success, the more likely it is that the CIO will be able to negotiate expectations in an informed and rational manner and deliver them."*

When probed as to what he meant by "IT literacy" we began to get a sense of the elements that make up the FoR, particularly the assumptions that are held in respect of information and technology. It is a recognition of how information and technology can impact organizational performance, both operationally and strategically. In addition, it is about understanding how IT generates business value and what the role of non-IT executives is in that quest. The FoR also determines the extent to which the CxO leadership team engages in IT matters: both in the IT decision-making processes, such as prioritization and portfolio management, and in the IT value creating process itself. Without an appropriate FoR, the CIO is often left to his/her own devices, and with little engagement from peers there is likely to be misalignment of expectations. One CIO recounted his experiences at a previous company where technology was very much a back-office function: *"The CEO always saw IT as a technological subject and struggled to talk to me about anything to do with the business and where it related to IT."*

There was a strong suggestion from that data that an inadequate FoR can have major business implications. As a Director of private equity firm noted *"many companies still don't yet see IT as a core, strategic driver of value in their business. As a result, they don't see the CIO role as being especially important. IT is seen as a hygiene factor—and only becomes an issue of importance when it stops working or goes over budget. It's not thought of in strategic terms; nor in terms of top line growth or bottom line performance. All of which means that there is limited understanding of the role of the CIO, and its potential importance to the business."*

The Director of a global investment bank was more somber in his assessment: "*There is little clear understanding of the role of the CIO—and its potential importance—because there is such limited understanding of IT as a discipline. The majority of executives have lamentable IT fluency—and don't seem particularly troubled by the fact. Yet they would never be so blasé about, say, a lack of understanding of finance or marketing—because they know they would be vilified by peers. Yet somehow, being ignorant about IT is not seen as a major problem for business people. Except of course it is.*"

Recounting his previous experiences in other organizations, the CEO of a European telecommunications company commented: "*In terms of enablers, I think the overall IT literacy of the senior management team is the most important. If the CIO and the rest of the management team can understand one another, then setting expectations is so much easier.*" This view was echoed by a partner in a global management consulting firm: "*If the other members of the senior management team have no understanding of IT or its power as a strategic lever, then the CIO has little hope of setting and managing expectations, or delivering against them. So IT literacy across the senior management team, and indeed the company at large, can be either a barrier or an enabler—though right now, for the most part, it's a barrier [in most companies].*"

Not appreciating the role that technology played was illustrated by a partner in a management consultancy firm who recounted the story of a recent assignment with a large fast-moving consumer goods (FMCG) company that had decided to sell off one of its operating companies. "*Unfortunately this strategy was not known to the CIO when SAP [its global ERP system] was implemented and, as a result, when they started the process of selling the company, they found that the IT system for that one operating unit couldn't be 'unplugged' from the rest of the organization. Potential buyers realized that they would have to create an entirely new IT system from scratch—and modified their valuations of the company accordingly. Very significant value was lost—simply because the Board didn't recognize the importance of involving IT when considering the long-term future of the company.*" A similar sentiment was expressed by the CIO of a large global law firm, who was not on the senior management team (he reported to the Director of Business Services), "*We're often involved far too late or in the latter stages and we're not hearing some of the early dialogue and then we're playing catch-up.*"

The consequence of not understanding what IT could potentially contribute or how IT generates value was starkly illustrated by the experiences of a CIO when he worked for a European Business Services company: "*I don't think they quite understood what my contribution could be. They didn't understand the business engagement side of IT and I spent quite a lot of my time selling that—the stuff like projects going live, the need for change management and the business ownership of IT solutions wasn't good. The expectation on me was to deliver but when I said I couldn't deliver successfully without you playing your role in this project, there was quite a lot of surprise."* Box 2.1 describes the experience of a CIO who worked for two different CEOs in the same organization.

Box 2.1   A Tale of Two CEOs

One of the CIOs interviewed worked for a European Business Services organization and experienced at first hand the impact of CEO IT savvy. When he was first hired, he reported directly to the newly appointed CEO of the company and was a key member of the senior management team. Prior to his appointment, IT only "looked after the plumbing". This new CEO was strongly of the opinion that information and knowledge drove the business and that IT offered opportunities to be exploited. He gave the CIO the mandate to drive a transformation and innovation agenda. However, not all of the senior management team were of the same view as the CEO; as the CIO recounted, the *"process of decision-making prioritization, governance around the value-add of the IT activity was completely new to them. They quite naively thought that if they asked IT to do something they would just do it and they didn't have to actually play a role. So [with the support of the CEO] lots of education about their role and what IT projects actually looked like. We had a hard and fast rule—every project had a project manager and a sponsor in the business who attended the weekly project meeting to try and have some rules and practical actions to underpin the education."* The CIO regularly interacted with customers and business partners and was party to discussions about potential acquisitions and part of all due diligence efforts. With the active support of the CEO, he introduced strong IT governance; the CEO chaired the IT Steering committee. Again, with the support of the CEO, he pushed responsibility for many aspects of IT out to colleagues from the business. No IT investment went ahead without strong business sponsorship. He developed a strong internal network and had credibility as a deliverer; although he would admit this was achieved as there was strong business involvement in all IT-enabled change projects (there were no IT projects!).

Four years into his tenure the CEO was headhunted to a new organization. His replacement had a completely different perspective on IT. He saw it as a cost of doing business, and, more strikingly, a cost to be minimized. He also brought some key executives with him and changed the reporting structure, with the CIO now reporting to the CFO and relinquishing his place on the top management team. The new CEO did not see why he should attend steering committee meetings, with the result that the CIO took over as chairman of this forum, although it very soon disintegrated as attendance was poor. Taking their cue from the CEO, the new members of the leadership team were reluctant to assume any responsibility for IT and were slow to engage with IT issues. To cap matters off, the CEO felt that the company was spending too much on IT and sought a significant reduction in the IT budget. The CIO saw the role as having regressed *"and this business about process, innovation and perhaps information is [now] not perceived as being a significant part of that persons [CIO] responsibility"*, although he was unsure where it did reside. He was at pains to point out that he didn't have a poor relationship with the CEO—he described it more one of frustration—but that the CEO *"saw IT as a technology subject and struggled to talk to me about anything to do with the business and where it related to IT."* Within months, the CIO had resigned.

If the strategy of the organization is strongly shaped by information and technology, the demands placed on the CIO will be different than those where IT plays a less central role. As a senior telecom analyst noted, "*if you think about it, the role of the CIO is defined by the business of the company. What I mean is that a CIO for a low volume, high margin fashion house is going to be very different from the role of a CIO in a major telecoms operator.*" However, this is a strategic decision that is shaped by the FoR of the leadership team.

As might be expected, the FoR also influences both the operating and organizing model for IT and reporting relationships. The CIO of a Media Group commented: "*I think many companies still see IT from the perspective of managing a cost base. And as a result, in many companies, IT is handled by a CIO who reports to the FD [Finance Director].*" The operating model for IT also plays a key role in determining the value derived from IT, and a lack of savviness can result in the adoption of a model that conflicts with the business operating model. The CIO of a European Merchant Bank found herself fighting running battles with country CEOs. The business was run as a multi-local operation, where country CEOs had full profit and loss (P&L) responsibility. However, the bank ran IT as a centralized operation with investment determined at headquarters and all development resource located at the center. With full P&L responsibility, country CEOs were reluctant to have IT systems imposed upon them by the center or indeed to fund centrally developed systems.

Expectations of CxOs for CIOs

We have already noted that CxO expectations are strongly influenced by the FoR of the senior leadership team. These expectations ultimately define the CIO role and the extent to which CxOs engage with IT issues. Our data reveals a potential gap between what a CIOs can expect the role to encompass and what the CEO/CxOs expect of the incumbent. One leading recruitment consultant expressed this succinctly when she noted that, "*most leadership teams [that she has dealt with] do not know what good is!*" She went on to explain that their expectations for a new hire are typically framed by their experiences and, to some extent, the previous incumbent in the role.

This sentiment was wryly echoed by the Group Finance Director of a global publishing and media business: "*One of the main reasons why there are so few CIO's in the UK is simply that very few Chief Executives have ever met or even aware of really good ones.*" From the data, it seems that senior executive teams err on the side of a technologist for the role. One of the CIOs interviewed, who has worked in the role for many organizations, noted: "*Where a company has never sampled anything different, then they naturally assume that this is what the CIO/IT director is all about [a technologist]. I have to say, when organizations like [his company] and others that I have been with, recognize that the CIO quite often doesn't actually fully understand or is up to speed with the technology, but fundamentally understands how to drive an IS organization towards the business benefits, the whole relationship changes quite significantly. That is why we're seeing that great difference.*"

From our interview data, it would seem that expectations are often framed by the historical experiences that CxOs have had with IT.[1] The Group CIO of a global transport company commented: "*You don't know something better until you see it. What I mean by that is there is a raft of CIOs out there in the IS community both in the UK and internationally that call themselves CIOs, but they're not CIOs. They are IT directors—there's a massive difference by that and they tend to be very technically focused, very operational focused, will drop everything as soon as a server goes down, still got their SMNs on telling them when their printer driver's not working—they are probably 95% actually operationally focused. Now if you bring that to the tables, senior executives of a company whether CEOs or CFOs, they can instinctively tell they're not talking the same language, they do not share the same mind space of what's going on and so they're seen as a service provider to the executive board of a company as opposed to someone who is part of the executive board of a company. That's the fundamental difference.*"

The lack of confidence in the IT unit's ability to deliver projects and services was seen as partially to blame. The CIO of a global insurance organization noted: "*Why would a company want an IT guy on the board when IT so consistently fails? Given IT's track record, companies are generally more comfortable with the CIO being a junior, apprentice executive.*" But of course this can be a catch-22 situation. Interviewees noted that failed projects and unreliable services often mean that business managers are reluctant to get involved in activities to improve success, resulting in difficulty to kick-start any recovery process.

The measures used by the CxOs to assess the performance of their CIO can be a useful surrogate for what they expect of the incumbent. Our interviews revealed that there can be a mismatch between stated responsibilities and expressed performance metrics. Most of our CIO interviewees reported a variance between their aspirations for the role and how their performance is assessed by their c-level colleagues, although most noted that this is changing. Frequently, CIO's reported their aspirations in terms of supporting strategy, crafting the business direction, identifying disruptive technologies and envisioning new opportunities enabled by IT. However, their performance is often assessed in terms of project delivery, application availability, network uptime and maintaining agreed service levels. As a former CIO of an international pharmaceutical business told us: *"unfortunately you are more often measured by… housekeeping rather than competitive performance, and largely operational at that."* The CIO of a large UK retailer noted that in general CIOs are *"judged in part by have they not 'cocked up'—operational stability is still key in retail."*

A leading European academic suggested that a CIO can assess how his/her contribution is viewed: *"if the CEO of your business unit is putting together people for golf and business discussion over the weekend, would he consider the CIO amongst one of those foursomes, not because the CIO is a golf player but because at the 19ᵗʰ hole, there's going to be a lot of business discussion and the CIO has to be a trusted member of the team—a colleague, not just a supporter of the team."*

Relationship Between CIO and CEO and CxO Team

The critical importance of the CEO-CIO relationship has been recognized for some time.[2] Our data also revealed this pivotal role as well as the relationship between the wider CxO team. It suggests that without these strong relationships, the CIO is likely to struggle. The CIO of a global bank emphasized this: *"I think it has got to be done [becoming part of the inner sanctum] by just building relationships and trust really. … I think, really, just to be seen as someone who can add value and get invited into the appropriate discussion. It's the personal gravitas and communication skills of the individual."*

We questioned as to why strong relationships are mandatory, the CIO of a global bank emphasized: *"to create the empathy of a shared agenda so the individuals on the top table will have their own agendas, the collective agenda, and the most important thing is that we, through that, create development plans and create handcuffs that meet the individual agenda and the collective one. I think the relationship enables you to have the discussion and makes the politics more benign."* The nature of the relationship is what ultimately determines the frequency and quality of conversations that take place.[3] One CIO we spoke to was at pains to stress *"that it's all about the conversation [with peers]"*.

The consequence of a strong relationship was captured by the CIO of a global pharmaceutical company who suggested: *"For big companies in the market where there are opportunities on the horizon [it may not be next year], being able to have a relationship with the senior business people that results in early definition of a solution for the business to prepare itself and take advantage of new opportunities."*

He emphasized that this relationship must translate into a trusted strategic partnership. For him, this means not just having "*a seat at the table*", but also "*a voice*". Commenting that the CIO must be a member of the most senior leadership team, he went on to tell us: "*if you're really talking about a strategic partnership, then I think you need a seat at the table otherwise the perception is always you're a supporting function, you're an order taker and not someone who's sharing in the agenda for strategic change within the organization. It's either are you a cost center or a business capability that can add value? There is evidence of companies in our sector where the CIO sits on the senior executive team where the contribution of IS is held in higher esteem.*"

The CIO of a global bank highlighted the pivotal role of the CEO in ultimately defining the relationship that CIOs have with the leadership team: "*I think the key is if the Chief Exec makes technology the common enemy and so is always, if only jokingly, talking down technology delivery and not understanding the delivery of anything in the technology space as a partnership. It is very hard to turn that round.*"

IT Decision-Making Processes

Our interviews show the crucial importance of involving business executives in IT-related decisions such as developing the strategy for technology, prioritization of investment spend and implementing changes.[4] Without this involvement and active engagement, CIOs and CxOs were unanimous that the CIO will struggle. Equally, the data revealed that the CIO has also to be closely involved in business decision-making. The CEO of a European Telecommunications company told us: "*Another important enabler is the extent to which the CIO is involved in decision-making. If the CIO is one step removed from decision-making, then he or she is always playing catch up—and IT is always on the back foot. Unless the CIO is fully integrated into the decision-making process, he or she is never going to be able to deliver against expectations—because those expectations will be set without the CIO's full involvement.*"

This situation was reinforced by the CIO of a distribution organization: "*Because the issues that the CIO could contribute cascade down, quite often too late, and are diluted in their expression to the CIO. The time for changing the thinking is then a little bit late. The time to influence the rest of management thinking has gone and you are kind of back tracking.*" The partner in a global management consulting organization suggested: "*When IT departments are not involved in decision-making, they are not able to meaningfully manage expectations. As a result, IT leaders tend to have to spend a lot of their time and energy fighting fires. Conversely, where they are involved in decision-making, they have the opportunity to design, plan and execute in a way that is tightly integrated and synchronized with the rest of the business. There are so many examples of IT projects failing completely, or coming in late, over budget and out of sync with the needs of the company. And this is a sort of vicious circle—the more IT projects fail, the less likely IT will be involved in decision-making, and hence, the more likely future IT projects will continue to fail."*

Why a CIO needs early involvement in decision-making was identified by the CIO of a global transport company: *"How you know you're doing a good job … is when senior members of the board [I'm talking from a CIO's perspective here] are phoning you and asking your opinion and asking you to join into discussions—that's really the critical area that I look at that tells me I'm getting it right and doing a good job and they're not phoning me up because their iPhone doesn't work. They're phoning me up because they're saying we're going to buy [company name] in North America and we're worried about how we integrate that. 'We need you' [that's the three words!] as a part of the team to determine how we can do that successfully and the discussions that you're having aren't about we need this number of servers or whatever else, it's about how are we going to manage this change both culturally with the people, with the unions, with whatever. When you're at that level of discussion, that's really the case to me that you're delivering significantly to an organisation."*

The director of a global investment bank suggested that CIO involvement in business decision-making is a good proxy for the extent to which IT is integrated into business activities: *"In terms of enablers, I think the most important is the extent to which IT is integrated into the rest of the business. To start with, IT has to be involved in decision-making, otherwise it tends to head off in its own direction. The more CIOs or their equivalents are involved in defining the direction of the company, the more they can meaningfully contribute to the performance of the business. The problem is, in many companies, IT is rarely involved in important decisions. And so it get condemned to a dynamic of project followed by project followed by project—many of which are fighting fires and plugging holes, as IT struggles to keep up."*

IT Value Realization Processes

The vast majority of the CIOs interviewed for our research stressed the key role of CxOs and other executives in ultimately realizing value from IT investments. Managing the change associated with IT projects and programs was emphasized time and time again by interviewees as the cornerstone of the value realization process.[5] For example, the global CIO of a manufacturing firm, who also sits on the board of the company, noted: "*IT is irrelevant without the business change to go with it.*" He recounted a recent implementation of Salesforce.com where promised changes in sales group employee behaviors didn't materialize and the project floundered. This sentiment was similarly echoed by many of those interviewed.

The CIO of a biotech company stressed: "*The … engagement of the business, particularly of the sponsors, in major change that they're advocating through the organization. Getting the message across that we're in this together in implementing any change and fundamentally it's not done by IT it will be down to the business. If the business doesn't buy into that proposition, it isn't going to succeed.*" He went on to emphasize: "*Business commitment to the changes they have signed up for as in new projects rather than the operational stuff. … Around projects, the business committing the necessary resources for them to change. For example, while going through SAP replacement of JD Edwards and getting not just the people available but the best people out of the business to help with those transitions from one to the other.*"

Some CIOs went even further, highlighting that IT is ultimately a change function. The CIO of a global insurance organization emphasized: "*IT teams are meant to be delivering new value—it's a very different game to finance. Getting the accounting right, that is hugely important, it it's actually a clearly defined and relatively predictable process. IT is much more diverse, and far less predictable.*"

The CIO's Own Leadership Team

Interviewees were unanimous that the operational performance of IT does matter. As the CIO of a distribution company noted bluntly: "*Yes it's very hard to talk about innovation if the screens regularly go blank.*" Delivering operational performance gives the CIO credibility as they engage with business colleagues.[6] We will return to this point in later chapters.

In this regard, the importance of the CIO's own leadership team and the abilities of that team were stressed during the interviews. Ultimately, it is through this team that required IT capabilities are delivered. Perhaps the CIO of a UK police force captured this sentiment best when he noted he needed: "*A really great IT team to help [him] deliver.*" The partner in an investment bank who works closely with clients in merger and acquisition activity commented on his experience in assessing the IT capability of target companies: "*It's the capabilities of the individual [CIO] and the corresponding IT team that count.*"

The importance of this team to IT delivery was explained by the Head of Technology at a UK Retailer: "*I think he [the CIO] needs a really good manage-*

ment team to rely on; those people to take away some of the stuff that can clog up a CIO's work—if you're not careful it may mean you can't concentrate on some of the big issues. Another enabler—the quality of the staff generally in IT is important as well—you need to know you have the right skills. Whether sourcing internally or externally, you need to be able to rely on these people."

Given the time that CIOs spend on working with business colleagues, with vendors, customers, ecosystem partners, etc., the need for a strong leadership team was stressed by many of the interviewees. The CIO of a media group elaborated on this point: *"Speaking personally, I probably spend about 60% of my time working on plans for the future, and 40% on day-to-day operational issues."* He estimated that approximately 80% of his time was spent *"away from IT"* and that he was utterly dependent on his team.

This latter point was emphasized by most of the interviewees, with CIOs acknowledging the quality of their own leadership team having a major impact on what they can and cannot achieve. The CIO of a public sector/property management organization emphasized the *"[q]uality of individuals within my team. Having very good knowledge of technical and information delivery and having the ability to deliver those. Also being able to work with the business and talking to people within the business at their level."*

Despite this dependency, many of the CIOs interviewed experienced problems in hiring senior staff with the right skills, experience and attitude for their own leadership team. The CIO of a global insurance company told us: *"It's difficult to find enough people with the right mix of skills—the deep technology understanding combined with broad commercial acumen."* The CIO of a global manufacturing company recounted his experiences: *"I've had some major problems recruiting the people who I think are capable of delivering on a strategy. The IT world is still full of infrastructure people. It's all well and good to have a chosen few shouting from the rooftops effecting change, but I've struggled with the ability of a wider theme to deliver. It has a knock-on effect on credibility of course, I think the CIO's never going to be effective until he brings his own team along. That's difficult."*

In a similar vein, the majority of the CIOs interviewed stressed the importance of building and developing their own team. The recently retired CIO of a global pharmaceutical company recommends CIOs to spend at least 25% of their time with their own direct reports. This he saw as necessary to *"grow great performers"*. Given that the CIO will be spending considerable time with business colleagues as well as with customers and business partners, these conversations need to be translated into work requirements. The clear message from our data is that a CIO is only as good as the team that surrounds him/her, so it is of upmost importance to get it right.

Implications for the CIO Taking Charge

A key question that must be asked is whether a CIO can actually make a material contribution to the performance of a company? In response to this question, the partner in an investment bank noted: "*Well to the extent that any member of an executive management team can, yes. But then it's very rare for a specific individual to have a profound impact on the performance of a company; it's usually teams who make a difference.*" The message loud and clear from the interviews is that it cannot be a solo run. What, therefore, can a CIO offer? In response to this question, the CIO of a distribution company suggested: "*New thinking about processes, different ways of doing business, better integration of business processes, better use of technology, better focus on business benefits and outcomes.*" Promoting and facilitating this dialogue can help in the CxO team in framing the vision for IT. Creating an awareness of risk is also seen as an important function of a CIO.[7]

However, one interviewee cautioned: "*[c]ompanies need to know how to use a CIO—what outputs they should expect, what contribution to the bottom line and so on. You can illustrate this problem quite clearly by thinking about a listed company doing an analyst or investor meeting. Generally speaking, the CEO will know how to direct questions to the CFO, the CMO and so on. But I don't think the same would be true with regard to the CIO—because I don't think enough CEOs really understand what the CIO contributes—in theory and in practice.*" As the model demonstrates, the lack of IT savvy across the top team can impact how the CIO role is defined and the expectations for the incumbent.

In his bestseller *Outliers*,[8] Malcolm Gladwell argues that success (and failure) is usually not defined or shaped by a single event but can usually be traced to the confluence of a number of factors. Our research strongly suggests that the same logic applies to CIOs, their effectiveness and ultimately the impact of information and technology on business performance. Our data reveals that it is not just about an incumbent in the position possessing the "right" competencies, these are necessary but not sufficient. Other factors also influence the ability of the CIO to get things done; or more correctly, the ability of the organization to optimize value from IT. The findings from this research emphasize that this quest cannot be enshrined in an individual role but demand a collective responsibility from all in the C-suite.[9]

What the research also indicates is that focusing solely on personal competencies for the CIO role is likely to be a fruitless endeavor. While possessing these competencies is obviously important for a CIO, it is unlikely these are any different from those required for other leadership roles. This also suggests that focusing solely on the role (i.e. of the CIO) is unlikely to result in much progress; much of the contemporary research explores the evolving role of the CIO. More fruitful is to begin with what is being sought, that is, optimizing business value through IT, and examine how the CIO and senior leadership team as a unit can contribute to this quest.

Perhaps the most clear-cut finding from the research is that hiring the "right" man or woman for the job and expecting that any historical problems with IT will just disappear is based on a false hope. The data reveal that central to the success of the CIO is the FoR of the CEO and CxO team in respect of what it takes for success with information and technology.[10] The implication is that before hiring a new CIO, the CxO team should take a close look at the environment within which he/she will operate. This FoR leads to the development of a shared vision[11] across the organization, which is key to achieving alignment with the priorities of colleagues[12] and ultimately optimizing the value from technology investments.[13] This poses a potential catch-22 situation: the leadership team realizing that there is a problem and that they are part of the problem!

The model we presented at the beginning of the chapter highlights that this FoR influences the role of IT in the strategy of the organization and the IT operating model. It also sets CxO expectations for the CIO role, frames the CEO relationship with the CIO and impacts CxO involvement and engagement in IT decision-making process, as well as in IT value realization processes. This observation is made despite the fact that research has long highlighted the key role of top management involvement in IT success.[14] While the research reported here identifies the factors that the FoR impacts, it seems that CxO savvy has not improved over the years. This situation must raise serious questions about the content of MBA programs and the focus of corporate executive development efforts. The problems that most organizations encounter with IT are less about the CIO and more about the shortcomings of CEOs and CxOs.

While this research is clear that the leadership of IT is no different than the leadership one would expect at the top of the organization, it does highlight a number of specific *leadership challenges* that a CIO faces. In taking charge, the newly appointed CIO should be cognizant of these.

The first is securing the engagement and active involvement of business colleagues in IT issues, particularly in decision-making concerning information and IT and IT value realization. If this is not forthcoming, generating value through IT, via IT-enabled change projects and programs, will be severely compromised. This quest demands a collective responsibility. This is perhaps the most demanding of challenges to overcome as it requires deeply held beliefs and assumptions to be overcome. As the interviews reveal, IT continues to be seen as a technical issue not a business imperative.

A second challenge is demonstrating and proving value from IT spend. The data highlighted that this can be a major task. A director of a private equity firm captured this challenge succinctly when he noted: "*It's still very difficult to measure the effectiveness of IT. Certainly within the context of due diligence, assessing IT is the most frustrating and complex piece.*" There are so many variables that can influence business outcomes and it is difficult, if not impossible, to isolate the IT contribution. The easiest measures to put in place relate to the performance of technology, such as uptime and availability; however, these are necessary and but not sufficient. Today, most firms could not function without their IT systems so there must be some value accruing from IT investments. However, establishing appropriate metrics to report this value remains elusive.

A third challenge is building a shared vision for information and technology. A leading European IS academic expressed this as "*a vision of how [IT] resources can be leveraged and utilized beyond simply competitive necessity*". In addition, the CIO must galvanize support among the CxO team as well as within his own leadership team around this vision.[15] Here, the CIO and CEO must work as one as it is normally expected that this vision will come from the CEO, although the CIO can help in framing it.[16]

This latter point emphasizes the critical importance of the CIO having conversations that matter. As Peter Keen emphasized: "*[a] CIO is brought into those conversations when he or she adds something relevant but different. The relevance comes from ideas, knowledge and expertise that relate directly to the critical business agenda, and the difference is in the distinctive IT-flavored perspective on the area of concern or opportunity.*"[17]

A final challenge for the CIO is building his/her own leadership team. There was unanimous agreement across the CIOs interviewed that they are only as good as their team. There was also a suggestion that CIOs often don't recognize the time and effort required to build, develop and nourish this team. A number of CIOs lamented the challenge of finding talent with the right blend of skills, competencies and experience for leadership roles in the IT organization. The majority of the interviewees advised that, if possible, the CIO should look to build his/her own team rather than expect to hire direct from the market. Obviously, for skills around cloud computing and security it may be more prudent to go directly to the market.

Whether these challenges will pervade into the future is anyone's guess. There was a suggestion by a number of those interviewed that as we move into the future, these challenges will be lessened as the C-suite develop an appropriate FoR. As the CIO of publishing/media organization noted: *"as a function of time, I think it will be less and less acceptable for other board members to know little or nothing about IT—particularly in industries where IT is important. I think board members will need to educate themselves about IT, because it has the potential to impact every other area of the business from marketing through to production and finance. It won't be acceptable for board members to glaze over."*

Notes

1. In the academic management literature this is often referred to as *path dependence*. For more on path dependence, see M. Stack and M. Gartland, 'Path creation, path dependency, and alternative theories of the firm', *Journal of Economic Issues*, Vol. 37, No. 2, 2003, pp. 487–494 and P. David, 'Clio and the economics of QWERTY', *American Economic Review*, Vol. 75, No. 2, 1985, pp. 332–337.
2. See D.F. Feeny, B.R. Edwards and K.M. Simpson, 'Understanding the CEO/CIO relationship', *MIS Quarterly*, Vol. 16, 1992, pp. 435–448; M.C. Jones, G.S. Taylor, B.A. Spensor, 'The CEO/CIO relationship revisited: An empirical assessment of satisfaction with IS', *Information Management*, Vol. 29, No. 3, 1995, pp. 123–130; A.M. Johnson and A.L. Lederer, 'CEO/CIO mutual understanding, strategic alignment, and the contribution of IS to the organization', *Information Management*, Vol. 47, No. 3, 2010, pp. 138–149 and A.M. Johnson and A.L. Lederer, 'IS strategy and IS contribution: CEO and CIO perspectives', *Information Systems Management*, Vol. 30, No. 4, 2013, pp. 306–318.
3. See A.M. Johnson and A. Lederer, 'The effect of communication frequency and channel richness on the convergence between chief executives and chief information officers', *Journal of Management Information Systems*, Vol. 22, No. 2, pp. 227–252.
4. Ross and Weill suggest six decisions traditionally made by CIOs that are really business decisions. See J. Ross and P. Weill, 'Six IT decisions your IT people shouldn't make', *Harvard Business Review*, November, 2002, pp. 84–92.
5. This is supported by research. See J. Peppard, J. Ward and E. Daniel. 'Managing the realization of business benefits from IT Investments', *MIS Quarterly Executive*, 2007, Vol. 6, No. 1, pp. 1–11; R. Ryan Nelson, 'IT project management: Infamous failures, classic mistakes and best practices', *MIS Quarterly Executive*, Vol. 6, No. 2, 2007, pp. 67–78; M.L. Markus, S. Axline, D. Petrie and C. Tanis, 'Learning from adopters' experiences with ERP: Problems encountered and success achieved,' *Journal of Information Technology*, Vol. 15, 2000, pp. 245–265; D.A. Marchand, W.J. Kettinger and J.D. Rollins. *Information Orientation: The Link to Business Performance*, Oxford University

Press, Oxford, 2001; J. Peppard and J. Ward. 'Unlocking sustained business value from IT investments', *California Management Review*, Vol. 48, No. 1, 2005, pp. 52–70 and J. Thorp, *The Information Paradox: Realizing the Business Benefits of Information Technology*, McGraw-Hill, 1999.

6. D. Marchand, 'The role of the chief information officer: Achieving credibility, relevance and business impact', in P. Bottger, ed., *Leading in the Top Team: The CXO Challenge*, Cambridge University Press, Cambridge, 2008, pp. 204–222.

7. For more on the risks associated with IT see G. Westerman and R. Hunter, *IT Risk: Turning Business Threads into Competitive Advantage*, Harvard Business School Press, Boston, MA, 2007.

8. M. Gladwell, *Outliers: The Secrets of Success*, Little Brown and Company, 2008.

9. J. Peppard, 'The conundrum of IT Management', *European Journal of Information Systems*, Vol. 16, 2007, pp. 336–345. See also D. Lohmeyer, S. Pogreb and S. Robinson, 'Who's accountable for IT?' *The McKinsey Quarterly*, 2002, Special Edition, Technology.

10. A similar conclusion was reached by Feeny and colleagues many decades ago when they reported that "*[t]he single most powerful discriminator in our study was that labelled 'CEO attitude toward IT'*". Some things never change! See D.F. Feeny, B.R. Edwards and K.M. Simpson, 'Understanding the CEO/ CIO relationship', *MIS Quarterly*, Vol. 16, 1992, pp. 435–448.

11. In their study of IS-business alignment, Tan and Gallupe report that "*there is a strong link between business IS-alignment and shared cognition between business and IS executives … Business and IS executives in the companies that report a higher level of business-IS alignment do have a set of core beliefs in common regarding IS.*" From their research Reich and Benbasat conclude "*[t]he one construct that seemed to predict long-term alignment was shared domain knowledge … The most important direct predictor of alignment in this study was a high level of communication between IT and business executives.*" See F. Tan and R.B. Gallupe, 'Aligning business and information systems thinking: A cognitive approach', *IEEE Transactions on Engineering Management*, Vol. 53, No. 2, 2006, pp. 223–237 and B.H. Reich and I. Benbasat, 'Factors that influence the social dimension of alignment between business and information technology objectives', *MIS Quarterly*, Vol. 24, No. 1, 2000, pp. 81–113.

12. D. Preston and E. Karahanna, 'How to develop a shared vision: The key to strategic alignment', *MIS Quarterly Executive*, Vol. 8, No. 1, 2009, pp. 1–8.

13. J. Peppard and J. Ward, 'Unlocking sustained business value from IT', *California Management Review*, Vol. 48, No. 1, 2005, pp. 52–70.

14. This sentiment echoes findings from research undertaken in the early 1990s, where the "*critical dependency for the CIO is the attitude and influence of the CEO*". See M.J. Earl and D. Feeny, 'Is your CIO adding value?' *Sloan Management Review*, Spring, 1994, pp. 11–20. See also earlier studies:

W.H. Doll, 'Avenues for top management involvement in successful MIS development', *MIS Quarterly*, Vol. 9, No. 1, 1985, pp. 17–35; J.T. Garrity, 'Top management and computer profits', *Harvard Business Review*, Vol. 41, No. 4, July–August 1963, pp. 172–174; S. Jarvenpaa and B. Ives, 'Executive involvement and participation in the management of information technology', *MIS Quarterly*, Vol. 16, No. 2, 1991, pp. 205–227; A.L. Lederer and A.L. Mendelow, 'Information systems planning: Top management takes control', *Business Horizons*, Vol. 31, No. 3, 1988, pp. 73–78; J.F Rockart and A.D. Crescenzi, 'Engaging top management in information technology', *Sloan Management Review*, Summer, 1984, pp. 3–16 and T.C. Willoughby and R.A. Pye, 'Top managements' computer role', *Journal of Systems Management*, Vol. 28, No. 9, 1977, pp. 10–13.

15. H.G. Enns, D.B. McFarlin and S.L. Huff, 'How CIOs can effectively use influencing behaviors', *MIS Quarterly Executive*, Vol. 6, No. 1, 2007, pp. 29–38.

16. A similar sentiment was expressed by James Emery in an editorial commentary in *MIS Quarterly* back in 1991. See J.C. Emery, 'What role for the CIO?', *MIS Quarterly*, Vol. 5, No. 2, 1991, pp. vii–ix. For a framework to help build a shared vision, see D. Preston and E. Karahanna, 'How to develop a shared vision: The key to IS strategic alignment', *MIS Quarterly Executive*, Vol. 8, No. 1, 2009, pp. 1–8.

17. 'Engaging in CIO-CxO "Conversations that matter": An interview with Peter Keen', *MIS Quarterly Executive*, Vol. 9, No. 1, 2010, pp. 61–64.

3

How New Leaders "Fit In"

An executive's transition into any leadership role can be a challenge, for both the executive themselves and the host organization. Such transitions do not always go smoothly, and the negative consequences can be significant for everyone concerned. Having looked at the key contextual factors that can influence the performance of the incumbent in the CIO role, this chapter explores research that has studied how new leaders "fit in" to an organization. This is particularly pertinent when the CIO comes from outside the organization but is equally relevant for an inside appointment as it speaks to how an executive can shape their role.

In this chapter we review research that has explored how organizations and individuals negotiate the dynamics of fitting into a new role. In particular, we look at two theories that are of relevance: role theory and leader socialization theory. Both inform what happens when a new CIO turns up to take up their position, and importantly, what a CIO can do to transition in a smooth fashion.

Role Theory

We saw in Chap. 1 that members of a senior leadership team can have diverse views of the CIO role depending upon their frame of reference (FoR) and the assumptions that reflect their views on information and IT, how both should be managed and what it takes for an organization to be successful in harnessing the capabilities of technology. These assumptions include who sets IT direction, how central information and technology are to strategic ambitions, the value placed on IT knowledge, justifications required for IT investment,

© The Author(s) 2020
T. Gerth, J. Peppard, *Taking the Reins as CIO*,
https://doi.org/10.1007/978-3-030-31953-3_3

where accountabilities should lie and how benefits from IT investments are realized.[1] Ultimately, the FoR will determine the CIO's status and likely influence that they have in the organization. But this is only part of the story.

Organizations are social systems subject to the vagaries of human behavior. Organizational role theory is a version of role theory focused on social systems.[2] This is the domain of the CIO and it provides insight into the CIO's role experience. A popular model of how individuals take on organizational roles was first introduced by scholars Daniel Katz and Robert Kahn.[3] Their model describes a dynamic interaction between "role-senders" who communicate organizational expectations of a role and the "focal person" who occupies the role. The theory presumes that expectations are a major generator of roles, but does not presume congruence between expectations and performance. This points to the fact that executive performance should not be simply a function of what executives *do*, but what they *do* compared to what is *expected*.[4] The executive has some influence on these expectations in a way and an extent that subordinates do not. In general, the higher in the organizational hierarchy an executive sits, the more influence they have on their actions.

For a newly appointed CIO, it highlights the importance of understanding what is expected of them in the role in terms of achievements. In short, it paints a picture of what "success will look like". At the same time, the CIO also needs to be cognizant of the cultural context of the organization as this should frame how they achieve results. One CEO described a CIO who had worked for him as someone you could depend on to get the job done, but there would be a lot of casualties along the way, which was not the usual approach in the organization.

In role theory, the concept of "enactment" captures the notion of an executive actively and deliberately creating the environment rather than solely reacting to it.[5] This concept was embraced by one researcher by including *choices* in a model of executive behavior: demands, constraints and choices.[6]

Demands are what anyone in the job *has* to do. Demands are what must be done, not what ought to be done or what the CEO thinks is important. For a CIO, this might be overhauling legacy systems or reducing costs.

Constraints are the factors, internal or external to the organization, that limit what the executive can do.

Choices are the activities within the executive's control, for example:

- How work is accomplished
- What work is accomplished (i.e. priorities)
- What and how to delegate work to others
- How and when to participate in organizational activities

These *choices* are how an executive can influence their job rather than just reacting to the demands of others and the usual organizational constraints (e.g. resource limitations, financial, legal, technology, etc.). Another model of "expectation enactment" describes the dynamics of how an executive can modify the expectations others hold for the role.[7] In other words, to close a gap between what is expected and what the executive does. This does not presume that the executive is not doing what is required, but rather, has influence over setting the expectations to begin with. We saw that an executive FoR can influence expectations; sometimes CIOs might feel that colleagues FoR need to be amended to re-align expectations. This points to the importance of ensuring there is alignment between the expectations of the leadership team, particularly the CEO and CIO.

Another useful model describes a *role-individual-system* triangle with the "ideal role" is what connects the individual and the organization.[8] Often, when considering how executives fit in, the focus is strictly on the person's individual traits and how the organization operates. "Role" in the triangle model is a way to connect the dots for role expectations with the executive's control over how they do the job.

We saw in Chap. 1 that a contributor to the ambiguity around the CIO role is because there are different "types" of CIO roles which primarily depend on the situation and circumstances that exist in the organization at a point in time. Role theory suggests that these factors will be taken into account by the organization's role-senders (primarily the CEO and executive team) who will communicate those expectations to the CIO (focal person). A gap in understanding is possible between the two parties resulting in role conflict and ambiguity. Research has identified that building a shared understanding of the role is critical to a CIO's effectiveness.[9]

Chapter 2 presented a model describing the factors that can influence a CIO's performance in the role. What an executive can do is a function of both the organizational context and executive's competence, rather than the latter alone. This systematic perspective is much more dynamic than a static matching of the role as defined by the organization and the individual personality traits hoping for a match.

Ultimately, how a CIO fits in to the organization is, to a large degree, dependent on how they meet expectations. The CIO role set can be used to describe how people inside and outside the organization influence the role. People who influence the CIO's role are considered "role-senders" because they communicate something about role expectations to the CIO. Figure 3.1 below shows a typical CIO's role set, assuming the CIO reports to the CEO.

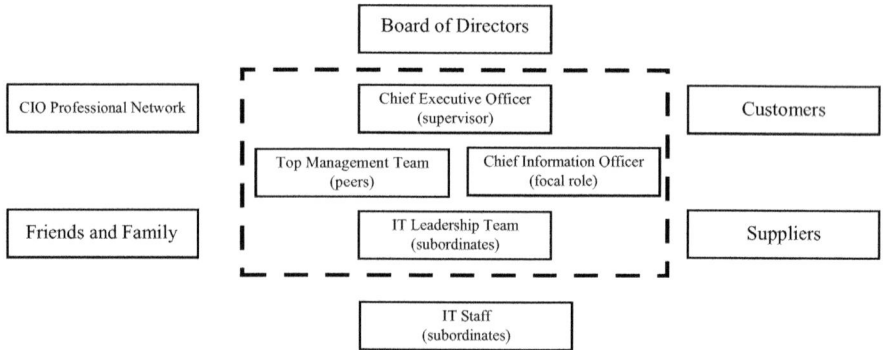

```
                          ┌─────────────────────┐
                          │  Board of Directors │
                          └─────────────────────┘
┌──────────────────────┐   ┌─────────────────────┐   ┌──────────────┐
│ CIO Professional     │   │ Chief Executive     │   │  Customers   │
│ Network              │   │ Officer (supervisor)│   │              │
└──────────────────────┘   └─────────────────────┘   └──────────────┘
                   ┌──────────────┐ ┌─────────────────┐
                   │ Top Management│ │ Chief Information│
                   │ Team (peers)  │ │ Officer (focal   │
                   └──────────────┘ │ role)            │
┌──────────────────────┐ ┌─────────────────────┐   ┌──────────────┐
│ Friends and Family   │ │ IT Leadership Team  │   │  Suppliers   │
│                      │ │ (subordinates)      │   │              │
└──────────────────────┘ └─────────────────────┘   └──────────────┘
                          ┌─────────────────────┐
                          │ IT Staff            │
                          │ (subordinates)      │
                          └─────────────────────┘
```

Fig. 3.1 CIO role set. (Source: Authors)

This model can be modified for those organizations where the CIO reports to another executive level. The CIO's immediate (inside the dotted line) and most powerful influences or role-senders are their "supervisor" the CEO, their peers and their leadership team of direct reports. Influencers who sit "outside the box" are much weaker than those "inside the box" on setting role expectations. In a later chapter we will discuss how the CIO's peers on the top management team perceive the role and what their expectations are for the CIO. A challenge that a CIO may have to navigate is that perceptions and expectations will not uniform across the top leadership team! The people that surround the CIO as role senders are influential and the CIO can exert influence on the role themselves (i.e. enactment), but that is still not the entire story for a dynamic process like taking charge. This brings us to the notion of socialization.

Organizational Socialization

Socialization is the process by which an individual acquires the social knowledge and skills necessary to assume a role in a particular organizational setting.[10] It essentially describes a process where "raw" newcomers are transformed into functioning members of the organization. Organizational socialization applies to many different types of organizations, including public sector, military, religious and political.

Socialization can also be seen as a process of mutual adjustment between the individual and the organization. It is the theoretical basis for understanding that the taking charge process is much more than role senders giving the CIO signals of what is expected that they accomplish. There is a duality at play where organization seeks to influence and shape its members while at the same time the individual is trying to define and shape his/her role within the organization.[11] Socialization refers not only to the adjustment to a specific organization but also to the learned behaviors from multiple career experiences in the case of a specific vocation or profession.[12] Role socialization specifically refers to this dynamic, for example, how the CIO learns to become a CIO. They may learn on the job, through education, have mentors, leverage a peer network and other ways. Our research focused on the organizational socialization rather than role socialization as we were interested in organizational adjustment rather than the career progression to becoming a CIO. Of course, we also assumed that, when hired, CIOs already knew enough of the role to get started.

The stages of the organizational socialization process have been studied by several researchers.[13] Proposed models focus on identifying the sequence and timing of stages through which an individual passes from being an "outsider" to becoming an "insider". In general, these models suggest three distinct phases. The first stage is where the individual prepares to join a new organization. The second is described as how the individual begins to understand their role and how the organization works. The final stage is when the individual becomes a fully functioning member of the organization. When we discuss our research findings for CIOs, you will see that we have also identified phases, although we don't want to reveal too much now!

Research into organizational socialization is concerned primarily with the actions that an organization can take to achieve certain socialization outcomes. Researchers have studied how different organizational experiences impacted newcomers' commitment over the course of their tenure with an organization and is built on the concept of "people processing".[14]

This research stream launched a plethora of studies focused on identifying what organization actions or tactics would bring about positive outcomes such as turnover reduction, job satisfaction, commitment and promotion.[15] It focuses primarily on the degree of individual conformity to the organization's demands and the resulting outcomes. It is a one-way perspective of how the organization can "process" newcomers. The weakness with this line of research for leaders is that it does not capture the leader's ability through the process to influence the organization as mentioned previously with executive enactment. Certainly, an executive like the CIO is not the same as a fresh college graduate. Recognition of the unique qualities of a new leader has led to a number of studies that focused on this socialization process.

Leader Socialization

Leaders bring a complex set of beliefs and assumptions built from previous experiences to a new appointment. Those having held multiple senior executive positions also bring a stronger set of expectations about the role than someone entering the workforce for the first time and tend to have more discretion in enacting those role expectations.[16] The previous experience of CIOs is a common variable in research with characteristics such as industry experience,[17] business knowledge,[18] IT experience[19] and previous experience in the role all used to study CIO effectiveness.[20] Industry experience and IT experience has been considered a positive influences on a CIO's effectiveness in these studies. However, our research shows that many contemporary CIOs are crossing industries and often come from a non-IT background bring a fresh perspective. One consistent conclusion from our research and others has been that a high level of business domain knowledge is linked to success as a CIO. So, the strong message is, if coming from outside the industry learn about it! Whether a person has previous CIO experience shows mixed results in terms of linkage to success. Executives new to the CIO role are often promoted insiders and have been successful because of other factors. As we noted in the previous chapter, experienced CIOs can switch organizations and fail miserably. We'll show evidence of both as we progress through the book.

Socialization theory is sensitive to the processual phenomena of a leader's adjustment to a new appointment. Socialization is an important process because even a CEO is influenced by the organization's belief systems and informal power structures. Moreover, no leader has total control of all aspects of an organization. From our experience, we would suggest the impact of organizational socialization on new leader transitions is under-emphasized in the management literature. However, there are three studies worth mentioning.

Probably the most significant study on leader socialization and taking charge was undertaken by John J. Gabarro.[21] Gabarro studied 14 cases of executives taking charge of new assignments. His key finding was that the executives all followed a similar five-stage process. These stages existed regardless of the succession type, organization size or background of the executive. An important implication of Gabarro's work was that it contradicted the concept of fast track one to two years assignments for executive development. It took almost three years (an average of 33 months) for the executives in his study to master a leadership assignment. A limitation of this research is that it does not capture the mutual adjustment dynamic, assuming that the executive generally has complete control over the transition. Ten years after Gabarro's seminal study, another study developed a theoretical model of CEO socialization and its influence on strategic change.[22] The model captures the combination of individual contribution to socialization and organizational influences.

One study worth noting is a single case study of the first two years of a new CEO's appointment as leader of a teaching hospital.[23] The authors develop a dynamic model of a mutual adjustment process. They contend that it is through the mutual adjustment process of leader socialization that convergence between the leader and organization occurs. It is this convergence, or lack thereof, that determines what the authors identify as four possible socialization outcomes. These outcomes are transformation, assimilation, accommodation and parallelism. "Transformation" implies that the new leader is successful in imposing his/her will on the organization. "Assimilation" implies that the leader will gradually adopt the organization's dominant beliefs and accept the role expectations of the other members. "Accommodation" implies that there is a mutual adjustment of beliefs and expectations on the part of the organization, its members and the leader. All three of these outcomes are considered to be forms of integration. The last outcome, "parallelism", is a condition where there is persistent divergence between the leader and organization and where integration does not occur.

A significant amount of research on executive transitions has been done by Michael Watkins.[24] While not specifically focused on organizational socialization per se, he has written and consults widely on making successful executive transitions. Our discussion in the next chapter on CIO transitions is built upon Watkins' work. His seminal book *The First 90 Days* focused on how executives can make a successful transition by focusing on nine key areas as follows:

- Preparing yourself: learn all you can about the new job
- Accelerate learning: focus on learning the organization's culture and politics quickly
- Match strategy to situation: select a strategy based on the business situation
- Negotiate success: building a relationship with your new boss
- Securing early wins: get early "wins" to build credibility and energy
- Achieve alignment: aligning strategy, structure, systems, skills and culture
- Build a winning team: a leader needs the right team to achieve ambitious goals
- Creating alliances: building relationships with influencers
- Managing yourself: creating and enforcing self-discipline

Many of Watkins' principles have emerged from our research on CIOs and how they take charge. We investigated the dynamics of socialization with a focus on CIOs because CIO-specific research was slim.

There has been one academic study that focused specifically on CIOs' transition into a new appointment. The researchers collected data from interviews with 36 CIOs about the first year they were on the job.[24] They found that the type of predecessor determined the new CIO's choice of an agenda for action, and whether it was radical or incremental. The authors describe different types of predecessors and link the new CIO's actions to those types. The focus was only on the first year and this may not have been long enough to examine the phenomena completely. This study also used the predecessor as a proxy for the "state of IT" in order to describe the organizational context in which the new CIO is operating. As we saw in the last chapter, whether the predecessor was effective or not often has to do with factors outside of his/her control. These same factors might influence a new CIO as well. All research has limitations (including ours), but this study was one that we built upon in our own research into CIOs taking charge.

Lastly there is guidance from industry publications and consultants that don't necessarily fall into either the organizational socialization or the academic research bucket. Their conclusions do not vary from what we've already discussed, although most only focus on the first 90–100 days of a CIO's tenure.[25] With our work we were much more interested in how CIOs were successful beyond the first 90 days and to go beyond checklists to understand the more complex process.

Why CIOs Can Struggle in a Leadership Role

There is one final aspect that we have found is crucial to how CIOs fit in and it has to do with how they interact and communicate with people. Our work with aspiring CIOs suggests that many have dominant innate preferences that shapes how they interact and communicate and that this can have implications for their leadership style and, consequently, their success when they move into a leadership role. While these preferences may be compatible with success in an IT management and technical role, they can compromise developing a successful leadership approach.

Since 2006 one of the authors (Joe) has run an IT Leadership Program, an executive education program that is targeted at developing the leadership capability of aspiring CIOs. Participants come from large and small organizations, both in the public and private sectors. During the second module of the program, there is a focus on raising participants' self-awareness. Research has shown that self-awareness is a critical trait of successful leaders.[26] Being self-aware means having a realistic assessment of one's own abilities, strengths and weaknesses and the empathy one has, particularly in considering others' when making decisions (and vice versa!). For example, not being self-aware can reflect in not recognizing when actions that feel authoritative are actually demoralizing, or not having an accurate "read" on how others are decoding the messages being sent.

To raise participant's level of self-awareness, a psychometric instrument called Myers-Briggs Type Indicator (MBTI) is used.[27] After working with a number of cohorts an extraordinary pattern became apparent that was rein-forced by data subsequently collected: of the 16 possible profiles, the majority of aspiring CIO attending the program had a particular profile. These innate preferences have particular implications.

There is a long history of research highlighting that we all have innate pref-erences and ways of doing things. Just like being left-handed or right-handed, these come naturally to us. For example, while some of us like to plan well in advance of a deadline, many others leave things till the last minute; some of us have messy offices while others are much more organized.

Of course, the "last minute person" can greatly irate "the planner", particu-lar if they are working in the same team.[28] So, your natural preferences can impact others. But if you are unaware of your preferences and their impact on others, this can be detrimental to your ability to get things done. Moreover, if you fail to recognize that others might be naturally different than you, you can interpret their behaviors through your own lens and view them as some-way dysfunctional. Our preferences have strengths but also weaknesses, but these weaknesses can be alleviated; but you must first be aware of them.

Yet, it is possible to develop weaker preferences, and while it may never be as comfortable as your dominant preferences, performance can still be at a very high standard. Many successful CIOs compensate for their weaker innate preferences by developing a self-awareness of these, using this as a foundation to build their leadership capability.

Identifying Your Interaction Preferences

MBTI assesses a person's preferences along four dimensions: where you get energy from, how you acquire information, how you make decisions and how you plan. Each has two possible positions, giving 16 types. The four dimen-sions of MBTI are summarized in Figure 3.2.

Extraversion (E)	Where you	Introversion (I)
Energy produced through interaction with the outer world of people and things	get your energy	Energy produced through inner thoughts and reflection
Sensing (S)	How you	Intuition (N)
Information gathered through the five senses. Focus on concrete facts and experiences that occur in the present	acquire information	Information acquired as patterns and hunch. Focus on big picture, inter-relationships, meanings, and possibilities in the future
Thinking (T)	How you make	Feeling (F)
Conclusions based on logical analysis. Focus on impartiality and objectivity	decisions	Conclusions based on personal values focus on empathy, harmony, and impact
Judging (J)	How you deal	Perceiving (P)
Focus on closure, predictability, planning, organization and control	with the outer world	Focus on adaptability, flexibility, spontaneity, and openness to new information

Fig. 3.2 Overview of MBTI preferences

When we examined the MBTI data from IT managers attending the IT Leadership Program, of the 16 possible types, 65% fell into one particular type: ISTJs (introversion, sensing, thinking and judging).[29]

ISTJs have a strong sense of responsibility and great loyalty to the organizations and relationships in their lives. They rely upon knowledge and experience to guide them and pay attention to immediate and practical organizational needs. Generally preferring to work alone, they can be relied upon to fulfill commitments as stated, and on time. Their colleagues would probably describe them as practical, pragmatic and sensible, but they can also be seen as detached, inflexible and overly serious. They strive for perfection and can be poor at delegation. Moreover, they have a tendency to get bogged down in the detail and sometimes criticized for failing to see the "wood from the trees".

Indeed, when CxOs are asked to describe a stereotypical IT executive, their descriptions usually mirror that of the dominant MBTI profile. "Needs to get out more" is a comment we frequently hear in relation to their CIO, a reference perhaps to their introverted nature. "Can't see the bigger picture" is another that is encountered, a possible consequence of their strong sensing preference. "If it's not on their plan, it's a no!" a likely reflection of their J preference.

Why IT Professionals Get Stuck

When the data was probed further, it revealed that the vast majority of ISTJs would categorize themselves as "career IT people" or IT professionals. Most have spent the bulk, if not all, of their working life in an IT role of some sort. They also tended to have studied mathematics, physics, engineering, computer science or another technical subject. These disciplines typically have their unique language, seek precision, are logical and have their own theorems with provable theories. Perhaps their MBTI preferences have caused them to study these subjects and select IT as a career, a nod to their preference for S and J?

Our findings suggest that as IT professionals progress in their careers, they can find themselves in a predicament. The very things that may contribute to success in a technology role can lead to a downfall in a leadership position. Role requirements differ dramatically.[30] Figure 3.3 illustrates a generalized career trajectory that many IT leaders follow (moving from the bottom of the triangle upward). Working below the "dotted line" is highly suited to their educational background and MBTI preferences and they can thrive in such settings. They can feel comfortable as much of the content of the job is controllable and, to a large extent, *prescriptive*: there are rules to abide by, standards to meet, processes to implement, policies to adhere to and best practices to follow. The work may be challenging but solutions can be developed through logic.

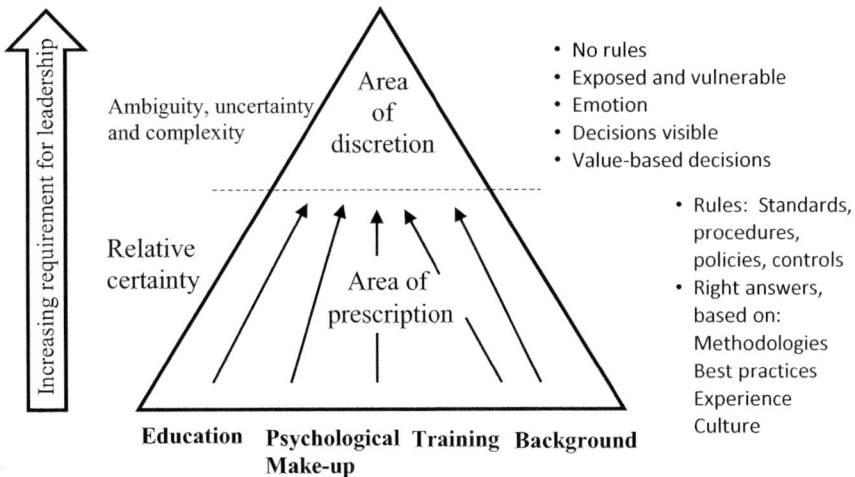

Fig. 3.3 Leadership, IT function and the career progression of an IT professional. (Source: Authors)

Career progression can see some move on to take on greater responsibilities through managing projects. Again, there are methodologies, supported by software applications, prescribing exactly how projects should be set-up and run and these are followed religiously. Even agile methods, such as SCRUM, have some structure to them. Others progress their career by remaining on the more technical side, perhaps assuming responsibility for security, infrastructure, telecommunications or data center. These latter roles require strong discipline.

The Challenge of Moving Up to Leadership Role

Operating above the dotted line is where the IT manager can struggle.[31] In a leadership role, they are now operating in an area of ambiguity, complexity and uncertainty. Politics is a matter of course. They now have considerable discretion in the decisions that they make and how they make those decisions. As such, they can feel exposed. The leader has to articulate a vision, galvanize support and take employees along with them. In the C-suite, leaders get things done, not because they are the boss, but through influence and working with others.

To succeed in these circumstances, it demands building relationships, navigating the political landscape, using influence and dealing with situations that can seem irrational and emotionally charged.[32] Moreover, as a leader you have lots of discretion—there are no manuals or methodologies providing guidance or vendor technical support to reach out to—you need to figure it out yourself. These messy surroundings are also the world of strategy, change and innovation. As an ISTJ, this can be a challenging and threatening environment.

After promotion to an IT leadership position many newly appointed CIOs struggle and revert to type, that is, back to being a technologist, making technology decisions, running IT projects and implementing service delivery processes. What they do not do is act or behave as a business leader; this might account for the high levels of attrition in IT leadership roles.[33]

Upping Your Self-Awareness Quotient

A preference for "Introversion" or "Thinking" doesn't need to keep you from becoming a great business leader; in the way that "Extraversion" or "Intuitive" doesn't guarantee success. It is about being aware of your own born-with preferences. By working on the opposite "handedness", aspiring CIOs are on the road to building their leadership capability.[34] Some suggestions:

1. Become more aware of your working and interaction preferences. Perhaps find your MBTI preferences. Understand the strengths and improvement opportunities of your profile.
2. Talk to your peers about how you come across and map against your MBTI profile. 360-degree reviews can give you a lot of information how you come across to colleagues.
3. Look to develop your areas of improvement. For example, with a preference for "Introversion", networking events are probably something you avoid, so attend one.

Any development activity will not be comfortable but with practice it will help you become a better leader ideally positioned to drive a digital agenda.

Fitting In

In this chapter we wanted to introduce you to research that lays the foundation for what we will be discussing in the remainder of the book that pertains specifically to CIOs. The first stream we discussed was role theory, a theory that describes how people's roles in organizations are shaped. We pointed out that in the c-suite, executives have more influence in how their roles are defined than others working lower in the organization who must primarily accept the organization's expectations. Organizational socialization describes the process of actions taken by the organization to shape how individuals fit into it. This process tends to be one-way; describing how the organization acts on individuals. Leader socialization is a much more complex process of mutual adjustment. The new leader must learn "how things are done here" in the organization in order to fit in. However, they also have influence over the organization and the potential to shape expectations of their role rather than simply "fitting in" to existing expectations. Finally, using a common psychometric instrument, MTBI, we presented an interesting phenomenon of a clustering of aspiring IT leaders in the ISTJ preference profile and how that might present challenges to fitting into a new leadership role. They key point is that whatever your preference, it does not constrain you being a great leader, but you must have this self-awareness and look to develop your weaknesses.

Notes

1. M. Kaarst-Brown, 'Understanding an organization's view of the CIO: The role of assumptions about it', *MIS Quarterly Executive*, Vol. 4, 2005, pp. 287–301.
2. B.J. Biddle, 'Recent development in role theory', *Annual Review of Sociology*, Vol. 12, 1986, pp. 67–92.
3. D. Katz and R.L. Kahn, *The Social Psychology of Organizations*, New York, Wiley, 1978.
4. C.P. Hales, 'What do managers do? A critical review of the evidence', *Journal of Management Studies*, Vol. 23, 1986, pp. 88–115.
5. K.E. Weick, *The Social Psychology of Organizing*, Reading, MA, Addison-Wesley, 1969.
6. R. Stewart, 'A model for understanding managerial jobs and behavior', *The Academy of Management Review*, Vol. 7, 1982, pp. 7–13.
7. N. Fondas and R. Stewart, 'Enactment in managerial jobs: A role analysis', *Journal of Management Studies*, Vol. 31, 1994, pp. 83–103.
8. I. Borwick, 'Organizational role analysis: Managing strategic change in business settings', in J. Newton, S. Long and B. Sievers, eds., *Coaching in Depth: The Organizational Role Analysis Approach*, H. Karnac Ltd., London, 2006.
9. For research into the social factors of a CIO's effectiveness, see H. Enns and S. Huff, 'CIO influence behaviors: Antecedents, consequences, and moderators', in Proceedings of the ACM SIGCPR conference on Computer personnel research, New Orleans, Louisiana, United States. ACM New York, NY, USA, 1999, pp. 194–199; H.G. Enns, S.L. Huff and C.A. Higgins. 'CIO lateral influence behaviors: Gaining peers' commitment to strategic information systems', *MIS Quarterly*, Vol. 27, 2003, pp. 155–176; D. Feeny, B. Edwards and K. Simpson, 'Understanding the CEO/CIO relationship', *MIS Quarterly*, Vol. 16, 1992, pp. 435–448; J. Peppard, C. Edwards and R. Lambert, 'Clarifying the ambiguous role of the CIO', *MIS Quarterly Executive*, Vol. 10, 2011, pp. 31–44; D.S. Preston and E. Karahanna, 'Antecedents of IS strategic alignment: A nomological network', *Information Systems Research*, Vol. 20, 2009, pp. 159–179 and B. Reich and I. Benbasat, 'Factors that influence the social dimension of alignment between business and information technology objectives', *MIS Quarterly*, Vol. 24, 2000, pp. 81–113.
10. J. Van Maanen, 'People processing: Strategies of organizational socialization', *Organizational Dynamics*, Vol. 7, 1978, pp. 18–36 and J. Van Maanen and E.H. Schein. 'Toward a theory of organizational socialization', in B.M. Shaw, ed., *Research in Organizational Behavior*, Greenwich, CT: JAI Press, 1979.
11. C.D. Fisher, 'Organizational socialization: An integrative review', *Research in Personnel and Human Resources Management*, Vol. 4, 1986, pp. 101–145.

12. D.T. Hall, 'Careers and socialization', *Journal of Management*, Vol. 13, 1987, p. 301 and J. Van Maanen and E.H. Schein, 'Toward a theory of organizational socialization', in B.M. Shaw, ed., *Research in Organizational Behavior*, Greenwich, CT: JAI Press, 1979.

13. B. Buchanan II, 'Building organizational commitment: The socialization of managers in work organizations', *Administrative Science Quarterly*, Vol. 19, 1974, pp. 533–546; D.C. Feldman, 'A contingency theory of socialization', *Administrative Science Quarterly*, Vol. 21, 1976, pp. 433–452 and E.H. Schein, *Career Dynamics: Matching Individual and Organizational Needs*, Addison-Wesley Pub. Co., 1978.

14. Ibid.

15. See the following for a survey of research tying organization actions to socialization outcomes: D.G. Allen, 'Do organizational socialization tactics influence newcomer embeddedness and turnover', *Journal of Management*, Vol. 32, 2006, pp. 237–256; N.J. Allen and J.P. Meyer, 'Organizational socialization tactics: A longitudinal analysis of links to newcomers' commitment and role orientation', *The Academy of Management Journal*, Vol. 33, 1990, pp. 847–858; B.E. Ashforth and A.M. Saks, 'Socialization tactics: Longitudinal effects on newcomer adjustment', *The Academy of Management Journal*, Vol. 39, 1996, pp. 149–178; B.E. Ashforth, D.M. Sluss and A.M. Saks. 'Socialization tactics, proactive behavior, and newcomer learning: Integrating socialization models', *Journal of Vocational Behavior*, Vol. 70, 2007, pp. 447–462; G.T. Chao, A.M. O'leary-Kelly, S. Wolf, H.J. Klein and P.D. Gardner, 'Organizational socialization: Its content and consequences', *Journal of Applied Psychology*, Vol. 79, 1994, pp. 730–743; G.R. Jones, 'Socialization tactics, self-efficacy, and newcomers' adjustments to organizations. *The Academy of Management Journal*, Vol. 29, 1986, pp. 262–279; A.M. Saks, K.L. Uggerslev and N.E. Fassina, 'Socialization tactics and newcomer adjustment: A meta-analytic review and test of a model', *Journal of Vocational Behavior*, Vol. 70, 2007, pp. 413–446.

16. S.J. Ashford and S.J. Black, 'Fitting in or making jobs fit: Factors affecting mode of adjustment in new hires', *Human Relations*, Vol. 48, 1995, pp. 421–437; N. Fondas and R. Stewart, 'Enactment in managerial jobs: A role analysis', *Journal of Management Studies*, Vol. 31, 1994, pp. 83–103 and S. Mantere, 'Role expectations and middle manager strategic agency', *Journal of Management Studies*, Vol. 45, 2008, pp. 294–316.

17. M.E. Porter, 'From competitive advantage to corporate strategy', *Readings in Strategic Management*. Palgrave, London, 1989, pp. 234–255 and Y. Zhang and N. Rajagopalan, 'Explaining new CEO origin: Firm versus industry antecedents', *The Academy of Management Journal*, Vol. 46, 2003, pp. 327–338.

18. D. Chen, D.S. Preston and W. Xia, 'Antecedents and effects of CIO supply-side and demand-side leadership: A staged maturity model', *Journal of*

Management Information Systems, Vol. 27, 2010, pp. 231–271; D. Preston, D. Chen, and D. Leidner, 'Examining the antecedents and consequences of CIO strategic decision-making authority: An empirical study', *Decision Sciences*, Vol. 39, 2008, pp. 605–642 and D. Smaltz, V. Sambamurthy and R. Agarwal, 'The antecedents of CIO role effectiveness in organizations: An empirical study in the healthcare sector', *IEEE Transactions on Engineering Management*, Vol. 53, 2006, pp. 207–222.

19. C. Armstrong and V. Sambamurthy, 'Information technology assimilation in firms: The influence of senior leadership and IT infrastructures', *Information Systems Research*, Vol. 10, 1999, pp. 304–327; H. Enns, S. Huff and B. Golden, 'CIO influence behaviors: The impact of technical background', *Information and Management*, Vol. 40, 2003, pp. 467–485; D. Preston, D. Chen, and D. Leidner, 'Examining the antecedents and consequences of CIO strategic decision-making authority: An empirical study', *Decision Sciences*, Vol. 39, 2008, pp. 605–642 and D. Smaltz, V. Sambamurthy and R. Agarwal, 'The antecedents of CIO role effectiveness in organizations: An empirical study in the healthcare sector', *IEEE Transactions on Engineering Management*, Vol. 53, 2006, pp. 207–222.

20. For a comprehensive review of CIO role effectiveness, see A. Hütter and R. Riedl, *Chief Information Officer Role Effectiveness: Literature Review and Implications for Research and Practice*, Springer, Cham Switzerland, 2017. See also M. Chun and J. Mooney, 'CIO roles and responsibilities: Twenty-five years of evolution and change', *Information and Management*, Vol. 46, 2009, pp. 323–334; D.E. Leidner and J.M. Mackay, 'How incoming CIOs transition into their new jobs', *MIS Quarterly Executive*, Vol. 6, 2007, pp. 17–28; J. Peppard, C. Edwards and R. Lambert, 'Clarifying the ambiguous role of the CIO', *MIS Quarterly Executive*, Vol. 10, 2011, pp. 31–44 and D. Smaltz, V. Sambamurthy and R. Agarwal, 'The antecedents of CIO role effectiveness in organizations: An empirical study in the healthcare sector', *IEEE Transactions on Engineering Management*, Vol. 53, 2006, pp. 207–222.

21. J.J. Gabarro, *The Dynamics of Taking Charge*, Harvard Business School Press, 1987.

22. N. Fondas and M. Wiersema, 'Changing of the guard: The influence of CEO socialization on strategic change', *Journal of Management Studies*, Vol. 34, 1997, pp. 561–584.

23. J.L. Denis, A. Langley and M. Pineault, 'Becoming a leader in a complex organization', *Journal of Management Studies*, Vol. 37, 2000, pp. 1063–1100.

24. D.E. Leidner and J.M. Mackay, 'How incoming CIOs transition into their new jobs', *MIS Quarterly Executive*, Vol. 6, 2007, pp. 17–28.

25. Some examples of this type of publication include K. Kark, M. Puranik, C. Dean and C. Brown, *The Essential Guide to CIO Transitions*, Deloitte Insights, 2017 and M. Bloch and P. Willmott, *The First 100 Days of a New CIO: Nine Steps for Wiring in Success*, McKinsey Digital, 2012.

26. See, for example, D. Goldman, 'What makes a leader', *Harvard Business Review*, June 1996, pp. 229–241 and G. Toegel and J.-L. Barsoux, 'How to become a better leader', *MIT Sloan Management Review*, Spring, 2012, pp. 51–60. Other traits include authenticity, expertise, presence, projection and networking. See, for example, A. Dale Henderson, *Leading with Gravitas: Unlock the Six Keys to Impact and Influence*, Rethink Press Limited, 2015.

27. MBTI is based on the theory of Carl Jung and his ideas. It gives us insights into how we may enhance our ability to do many tasks, in particular, interacting and communicating with other people. MBTI is not without its distractors; we use it in the classroom as a basis for introducing self-awareness. See R. Stein and A. Swan, 'Evaluating the validity of Myers-Briggs Type Indicator theory: A teaching tool and window into intuitive psychology', *Social Personal Psychology Compass*, 2019; e12434 and D. Pittenger, 'Cautionary comments regarding the Myers-Briggs Type Indicator', *Consulting Psychology Journal Practice and Research*, Vol. 57, No. 3, 2005, pp. 210–221. See also R.R. McCrae and P.T. Costa, 'Reinterpreting the Myers-Briggs Type Indicator from the perspective of the five-factor model of personality', *Journal of Personality*, Vol. 57, No. 1, 1989, pp. 17–40.

28. For more on working with people who are not self-aware, see T. Eurich, 'Working with people who aren't self-aware', *Harvard Business Review*, 19 December, 2018.

29. The data was collected from 264 participants, 22% of whom were female.

30. Ibarra and Hunter have noted that "*Many organizations still promote people on the basis of their performance in roles whose requirements differ dramatically from those of leadership roles.*" See H. Ibarra and M. Hunter, 'How leaders create and use networks', *Harvard Business Review*, January, 2007, pp. 40–47.

31. See A. Gerth and J. Peppard, 'The dynamics of CIO derailment: How CIOs come undone and how to avoid it', *Business Horizons*, Vol. 59, 2016, pp. 69–70.

32. A. Gerth and J. Peppard, 'How newly appointed Chief Information Officers (CIOs) take charge', *MIS Quarterly Executive*, Vol. 13, No. 3, 2014, pp. 159–173.

33. See 'CIO stats: Length of CIO tenure varies by industry', *Wall Street Journal*, February 15, 2017, available at https://blogs.wsj.com/cio/2017/02/15/cio-stats-length-of-cio-tenure-varies-by-industry

34. For some practical advice, see Morra Aarons-Mele, *Hiding in the Bathroom: An Introvert's Roadmap to Getting Out There (When You'd Rather Stay Home)*, Dey Street Books, 2017.

4

Setting the Stage for CIO Transitions

Chapters 1, 2 and 3 have outlined some foundational research and commentary on CIOs, highlighting the ambiguous nature of the role, presenting a model structuring the factors influencing performance in the role, as well as advocating taking charge as a process of mutual adjustment between the CIO and the organization. This material provides a broader context for what we will describe in the rest of the book, starting with this chapter. As emphasized in the preface, our objective with the research we undertook was to find insights related to how newly appointed CIOs successfully take charge so as to uncover what leads to effective transitions. In subsequent chapters, we will discuss the transitions, phases, activities and outcomes of the taking charge process, as well as present guidance that emerged from the research. This chapter is the start of that discussion with the focus being on the transition type, that is, the broad situation the CIO finds him/herself in on taking up the new assignment.

You will notice that from here on in, we isolate many quotes from our research interviews; we do so as a way of emphasizing what we were told during our conversations. As we mentioned in the preface, we want to give a voice to the CIOs and other executives who generously shared their experience and perspectives with us. They did so on the pledge of anonymity and we honor that by not identifying them by name. We will continue to share quotes like this over the next several chapters so that you can benefit from the full impact of their viewpoints and lessons. We hope that reading their perspective directly better illustrates the dynamics of the taking charge process.

At the end of this chapter we will share a few "CIO stories". These short vignettes will give you some insight into a small sample of the CIOs that

© The Author(s) 2020
T. Gerth, J. Peppard, *Taking the Reins as CIO*,
https://doi.org/10.1007/978-3-030-31953-3_4

contributed to our work. We've selected them because they are representative of those whom we've spoken to and worked with over the last ten years. A full compendium would be a book in itself. However, we hope that this selection brings them to life a little more for you.

Transition Types

Unless a start-up business, every CIO steps into an existing organizational situation when they take on the role and this situation can be described in terms of the transition type. The type of transition is a dimension of the organizational situation that signals an important context for the new appointment. The transition types described by the CIOs we spoke to were similar to those articulated by Michael Watkins.[1] Watkins described four types of business contexts that leaders, and specifically new leaders, find themselves in. We did not ask our CIOs to choose a transition type for us, but their descriptions of their personal transitions mapped directly onto the types described by Watkins.

Transition types for CIOs can be described as follows:

Start-up: the CIO is charged with assembling the capabilities (people, processes, information and technology) to get a new business, product and/or project off the ground.

Turnaround: The newly appointed CIO takes on the role in an organization that is experiencing problems with information and technology, with an IT organization that is "in trouble", and works to get it back on track. In this transition context, the perception of the top leadership team is that IT is not delivering to the extent that they believe it should, and the previous CIO was seen as having failed to meet expectations. This transition situation is often the result of a new CEO coming on board.

Realignment: The new CIO is hired to revitalize an IT organization that is "drifting into trouble". Prior to the CIO's appointment, tensions were beginning to emerge, often due to a new reporting line for the CIO, changes in the makeup of the IT leadership team or a new mandate for IT (e.g. a shift from cost minimization to a more strategic, customer-focused role). Given the new expectations, the existing IT organization was often characterized as "not fit for purpose".

Success-sustaining: The new CIO takes responsibility to preserve the vitality of a successful IT organization and "take it to the next level". The previous CIO was perceived as being successful and having performed well in the role and has either moved into a new role, to a new organization or retired.

What we found when we analyzed our interview data was that transition type directly influenced the *degree* of change that the CIO was required to implement, but did not significantly impact the phases of taking charge nor the timeline. CIOs reported similar phases and timelines regardless of the type of transition they were experiencing. We describe these phases and their timeline in detail in the next chapter.

Likewise, whether the incoming CIO was an insider or outsider also did not significantly influence the taking charge phases or timelines. An "insider" is an executive promoted from within while an "outsider" is hired from outside the organization. CIOs that took charge as insiders did not generally report accelerated taking charge timelines as suggested by a previous study of general managers.[2] For example, the insider CIOs still spent time early in their tenure building relationships with their top management peers. There are a couple of reasons for this. One reason for this was that insider CIOs typically have no previous experience in such a leadership position; this is usually their first appointment as a CIO. While they may have had some previous dealings with the members of the C-suite, the CIO role is a new one for them and therefore their relationship with this team has changed to one of a peer. This changed relationship requires them to build trust and credibility with their new role group. Insiders therefore still invested time in building those relationships and acquiring the knowledge specific for the functions, geographies or business units that were new to them. This is consistent with previous research into organizational socialization that suggests an individual will experience a period of adjustment even with the simple change of assignment, shift or location.[3]

Insider CIOs reported that they felt that their knowledge of the organization and its issues was beneficial to them even though this did not impact their taking charge process compared to outsiders as much as expected. This suggests that being an insider is an advantage for a CIO with no previous experience in the role whereas CIOs with previous role experience will be more comfortable as an outsider in a new appointment.

One factor that influences any person new to the job is how much advance visibility they have regarding role expectations and challenges.[4] CIOs varied in how much advance visibility they had to the issues that they would inherit in the new appointment. As one might expect, insiders expressed an advantage in this regard over outsiders. Two such insiders had interesting observations about their visibility into what they would face.

The first, the CIO of a semi-conductor manufacturer, was groomed for 16 years within the IT organization to become CIO. His appointment was not necessarily a surprise. As he described it:

We had a very active program for rotating high potential people across various disciplines in IT and after doing that for 16 years of my career, the seated CIO moved on and they came to me and said 'Okay, you're next in line.'

The CIO of a Pharmaceutical company was considered an insider because he worked as a consultant with his predecessor for several years.

I would say I did have a good view of what I was walking into. The size of the role I underestimated, but I was very much aware of what the issues were, where we had rubbed our customers the wrong way. And I was working with him [predecessor CIO] to try to correct the situation.

Even though this former consultant considered himself familiar with the issues, he still underestimated the size of the challenge ahead despite several years working with his predecessor. Nothing beats having to make actual decisions.

Another CIO, from an Electronics Distributor that was the result of a merger, described his experience becoming CIO, having already been CIO in one of two companies that merged.

I was involved, as CIO, in the due diligence process and integration planning. That made it easier in terms of coming in, because I could talk some of the language, not just generic business language, but very specific to the business of the other company.

Clearly, the insider CIOs felt that their transition into the CIO role was aided by the fact they knew the organization and its current issues. One insider CIO summed it up by saying:

I probably was 80% ready to hit on all cylinders. I spent 7 years prior working with the IT leadership team. CIO—Insurance Company

However, insiders tended to underestimate or simply be unaware of the breadth and depth of the role even though they were familiar with the organization. Insiders, in their previous roles, had not usually had the breadth of exposure that the CIO role entailed. Therefore, they still needed time to transition and build relationships with their c-suite peers.

These experiences were in contrast to how outsiders described their initial impressions. Acquiring accurate information in the interview process can be quite challenging, even when a high level of due diligence is exercised. Generally, CIOs reported mixed experiences. For example, one Consumer Goods CIO remarked about working with executive recruiters:

[W]hen you're talking to head-hunters about the types of things they look for in individuals, what comes through is their lack of understanding of the organizations they are working with and what would make a CIO successful.

Another CIO cautioned that this is not always the executive recruiter's fault since many CEOs themselves are not clear about the role when they described it to candidates.

Most CEOs would tell you they want a partner and they'll pump the job up a little bit to make it feel really strategic and the reality is … what they really want is an operator to contain costs. It is important that the business, the CEO, is clear. CIO—Electronics Distributor

These were common perspectives of outsider CIOs regarding the clarity of role expectations as defined by the CEO (and communicated through the executive recruiter). However, some outsider CIOs felt comfortable with the visibility that they had through the recruitment and interview process. An observation by the CIO of an air ambulance service was:

People made it very clear to me what kind of situation I was walking into. I think the company was very forthright and so I had a heads-up on most of the real problem areas.

Regardless of the amount of information attained during the interview process several CIOs experienced "surprises" to some extent or another. The reality is you just can't fully appreciate the situation until you start the job and there were many comments that reflected this perspective. The same Air Ambulance Service CIO recounted:

The picture painted prior to my taking the role … did not fully reflect the situation. You look down at a fire from an airplane and say wow! It looks pretty bad. But when you're down on the ground it's a different perspective.

The governance around the IT budget surprised the new CIO of a US Federal Government agency:

I think the biggest surprise … was the budget. I did not have a big enough budget at all. That was probably the biggest shocker and then the other was how much power the regions had.

A number of CIOs described situations far worse than they were able to discern in the interview process:

> When I arrived … it was far more urgent, complicated and dysfunctional than I had imagined even with a fair bit of due diligence. CIO—Hospitality Organization

> I had an idea of what it was like from talking to some of the business stakeholders. But one of the IT directors was protective of information and until he moved on it was very difficult to open the box and see inside. CIO—Casino Operator

> I don't think there is any CIO that can ever say that in the interviewing process anybody can tell you what really you would find coming in. Like the Wack-A-Mole game, knock down one thing but another thing pops up. CIO—Consumer Products Manufacturer

While a significant number of the CIOs we spoke to entered organizations from the outside and conducted due diligence regarding the organization's information and technology situation, to some degree there were always surprises. This was never described as deception on the part of the hiring organization but rather as a natural characteristic of the complex environment in which CIOs operate. Experienced CIOs, hired externally, understand the ambiguity of the role and the challenge of identifying the frame of reference (FoR) that ultimately shape the expectations of the CEO and other top executives. They worked on deciphering this during the recruitment process.

Most of the turnaround situations we encountered were a result of a strategic shift by the CEO regarding the role of information and technology. For example, moving from selling products to services and the new data-driven business models that this inevitably entailed. The others were reported as "IT is a mess, fix it" type turnarounds. Even in these situations, the "mess" often resulted from a lack of support by top executives to invest in IT and help make it successful; in other words, they were part of the problem. Lack of a strategic vision of the role of IT resulted in an ineffective IT function that did not serve the organization's needs. This may also explain why turnaround transitions were predominantly led by CIOs hired outside of the organization. It is not surprising that, given a turnaround situation, the predecessor CIO was viewed as ineffective and subsequently replaced.

Most realignment transitions are the result of a CEO who articulated a more strategic direction for information and technology. This new vision stemmed from different drivers such as a merger, geographic expansion or a renewed focus on customer engagement via technology. The majority of realignment transitions were led by CIOs from outside of the organization indicating that the predecessor CIO was not viewed as being able to make the required shift successfully and was replaced or demoted.

Succession-sustaining transitions do not consist of radical changes in strategic direction. These were transitions where the CIO was chosen primarily from inside the organization. This transition was characterized by a chief executive who wanted to build on the stability and success of the current regime. This is not to suggest that success-sustaining transitions are the same as having a strategic view of IT, only that it was perceived as successful in the eyes of top executives.

CIO Stories

The following "CIO stories" are short vignettes that describe the "taking charge" situations that some CIO encountered. We've chosen stories that present a cross-section of the CIOs who contributed to our research. These stories represent a combination of insiders and outsiders as well as transition types. Everyone's story is unique of course, but they do highlight the varied backgrounds and career paths that our CIOs followed. As will be apparent from these narratives, if not already, there is no standard template for success as a CIO.

Outsider Hired for a Turnaround Transition

The newly appointed CIO of a global apparel company faced a big challenge. He had previous experience as a consultant and as the CIO of another apparel company. He stated that "*IT needed a transformation*" in his new organization. A new CEO had established an aggressive growth strategy that included expansion in new global markets which "*required a whole new IT approach and mindset*", according to the new CIO.

He started by executing a rigorous on-boarding process of his own design, conducting interviews with the board, the top management team and his own IT leadership team. He addressed several challenges. The first was to refashion his leadership team. He sought to move it from focusing on technology to focusing more on business issues and priorities. However, there were many on the team who were not able to make that transition. He replaced almost the entire leadership team during the first year. This was followed by renegotiating existing outsourcing agreements that were too inflexible to support the new business strategy of speed and innovation. Another transformational approach was to start planning, measuring and evaluating the value contribution of each IT initiative rather than focusing only on cost, as was the case before he joined.

Because this CIO reported to the CEO, the focus on value raised his level of influence in the top management team. "*I spent two hours per week with the CEO talking about our operating model and the implications of what IT is doing on the business. It was extraordinarily helpful for me, and it's changed the way he talks about IT in our business.*" This CIO had gained legitimacy as a business leader who contributed to strategy. After three years as CIO, this executive was promoted into a broader role at the executive vice president level.

Insider Assigned to Realignment Transition

This insider was appointed as CIO of a company that manufactures premium fastening systems used primarily in commercial construction. He faced a realignment transition situation where there were pockets of broken areas that needed focus. He stated that the application areas were in good shape, but the infrastructure required some attention. One such area was helpdesk services: "*the CEO called me and said your first assignment is to fix our helpless desk.*" To improve infrastructure services, he initiated a process improvement program that significantly improved service levels. He assigned IT support staff to work in different parts of the business for short periods so that they built relationships with their internal customers and became more business-savvy. They reduced the number of desktop/laptop images from 37 to 4. He implemented more disciplined governance processes for technical change management. He also introduced customer service surveys and benchmarking.

He said that his promotion to the CIO role meant a significant change in his focus. "*The best advice I received was from the VP-HR, who told me I was no longer an IT guy, but a business guy.*" Even though he had worked in the organization for years prior to his promotion, he visited every top manager to build relationships that previously didn't exist and to understand their challenges. He had experience with the distribution function in his previous role but had not worked with finance, HR or the sales organization. These were all new relationships he had to build and functions he had to learn about. In addition, he had to win over several former peers in the IT organization who thought they should have become the CIO.

This CIO mentioned that after six months, he was feeling more confident about the role, but that it took him about two years to really be as effective as he could be. He benefited from the CEO's mentorship. "*The CEO really worked with me and for the first year, we had weekly meetings pretty religiously. But after that time, I think the confidence in me grew, and so we had these meetings less and less frequently.*" By all accounts, he was successful in his realignment transition. He was CIO for seven years before leaving the company to do consulting.

Outsider Who Led a Turnaround as a First Time CIO

This CIO joined the company, a consumer goods/lifestyle business, as a consultant with the objective of stabilizing a poorly adopted ERP system. He had extensive consulting experience with a Big Four practice as well as working in an in-house IT organization. He was asked to take over the CIO role and quickly found that the organization's technology issues went far beyond ERP stabilization. There were infrastructure, network and other performance issues that were not related to the ERP implementation. The situation also presented challenges in IT personnel, inadequate service delivery, lack of IT governance and poor business-IT relationships. This was clearly a turnaround transition, although not what the CIO expected!

The ERP issue was critical because the system supported the entire enterprise. The new CIO concluded that the cause of the adoption issue was that the IT unit pushed the new system on the business and the process owners were not savvy enough to understand the impact. With strong support from the Chief Operating Officer (COO) he quickly put a remediation plan together. "*When you come into this type of crisis situation you have to lay out a plan in layman's terms that is understandable. Top management needs to believe that if we execute on each of these items we will get out of this crisis.*"

After about one year the situation stabilized, and the CIO had earned the credibility of being trustworthy to deliver on his commitments. He pointed out that one positive was that the situation was so bad that he could only make it better! He was able to transition into a broader role as CIO to influence business strategy and technology driven innovation. He is still CIO at the company at the time of writing.

Industry Veteran Takes on a New Challenge

The CIO of this story had over 25 years of high technology industry experience before taking over as the CIO of high technology manufacturing company. At the time, he was in transition and considering retiring, but he joked that his wife was more interested in him taking a new role and getting out of the house! He was first interested in the job because the company was at the epicenter of some emergent technologies and had an aggressive growth plan. The CIO role reported to the CFO and after some due diligence he concluded that IT was going to be treated as a cost center and declined to move further in the recruiting process. Shortly after that the CFO left the company and the CEO realigned the organization so that the CIO reported directly to the CEO. The company circled back to our CIO candidate and he accepted the position after a good discussion with the CEO. The CEO admitted that they had been mistaken to align IT too far down in the organization and treat it as a cost center. He wanted to change that and position the CIO as a peer to the other top executives.

When the CIO joined the company and the new mandate for IT and reported structure was explained, the IT organization's morale increased significantly. In the opinion of the CIO, this was the first time that they felt they were valued. The CIO avoided calling his transition a "turnaround" and preferred to consider it as a "transformation". He had a good understanding of the situation at the company before taking the role because of his deep relationships within the industry. IT was viewed as just being the network "guys" and the CIO really worked to gain credibility for the IT organization with both executives and staff. He improved the IT governance processes by empowering managers, creating a technical architecture office and developing a priority planning process. He also implemented a full program management office and introduced CoBiT and ITIL frameworks.[5]

After only nine months the CIO was asked to give a presentation to the Board of Directors on IT risks and opportunities. This was an indication that IT was gaining visibility and becoming valued enough to get time with the Board. While the CIO was accepted to participate in strategy discussions, he felt it would still be 6–12 months before he really was driving the conversation with executives. During his interview with the CEO, the CEO told him *"What I want you to do is help us grow and avoid all the common pitfalls that so many Silicon Valley firms have made."*

From Production Supervisor to CIO

Starting her career in supply chain/operations was the platform for this CIO. Achieving the position of Director of Operations for a global food manufacturer eventually led to a role as an ERP program director. She then worked a few years at an ERP software provider, while a merger at her old company provided the opportunity to steer the merger integration and applications rationalization of the new entity. After that, she set her sights on a CIO role which she landed at another food manufacturer. It was especially appealing to her because it was a global role.

When she took over, the company had a "spaghetti applications landscape" similar to many global companies. There was little standardization and no long-term plan. Harmonizing the applications environment, setting technical standards and improving global IT governance were high priorities. Her approach was to consider these changes as organizational change management challenges. Rather than use the "bully pulpit" of the CIO role, she worked with executives so they understood the need for change and had input into what changes to implement. In this way she built a sustainable "business-led" governance of information technology versus a "CIO-led" governance culture. The IT governance processes became part of the overall enterprise governance. She worked on convincing her business colleagues to be more involved with IT governance at the same time as she enhanced the IT unit's influence on business strategy and direction.

In hindsight, her career appears well "architected". Starting off in operations/supply chain to learn the nuts and bolts of process and systems, then a stint at a major software company that led to a transformation leadership role that led to the CIO role. However, as she admitted, it was nothing of the sort! Each opportunity came along with the right role and timing. She simply took advantage of the opportunities that presented themselves and achieved a successful career.

An Insider from Finance Leads a Turnaround

This CIO's career started in a finance role for a retailer where she rose to the CFO position before joining a global oil and gas company where she worked in the finance function for 16 years. She was promoted to Director of Finance for the downstream business unit before being tapped to lead a business transformation initiative. At the time, the CIO teased her that someday she would be in his position. She would laugh at the thought, but very soon afterward landed the CIO role after a brief stint as the VP-Supply Chain.

When she took over the CIO role it had been vacant for nine months during a time that the company was acquiring another oil and gas business. Her description of the situation was "*it was not in a good place*". She had a jump on business partner relationships because of her work leading the business transformation program and supply chain. She was also aware of IT service issues based on her experience as an internal customer in the supply chain unit. Another early challenge was that reporting relationships were confused because of the merger activity. She re-organized in the second week because it was so dysfunctional. She terminated two people, promoted two people and everyone in her team changed roles except one individual. Now she had a group of leaders in place that bought into the key objectives. This team focused on improving IT service as well as moving forward with the IT integration tasks required by the acquisition. Another benefit of the re-organization was a more effective and efficient IT governance process.

She also helped her team transition from communicating in technical terminology to being more fluent and articulate in the language of the business. This significantly raised the IT savvy of her business colleagues. It also raised the business credibility of the IT organization in a way that provided legitimacy in participating in business strategy discussions. After stabilizing the IT organization, she introduced a formal competency model to use for talent management. This insider from outside IT built an effective organization based on her previous experience and leadership skills.

An Automotive CIO Moves to Turnaround Local Government

This CIO worked for 20 years in the automotive industry for two global companies located in the Midwestern US. He had 25 years of IT experience including 5 years at the CIO level before moving into the public sector. When the automotive industry waned, he started looking for a CIO opportunity and one came up in a local government in the southern US. He relocated his family but after 2.5 years they decided that the size of the city was not for them. He was recruited to return to their hometown to be the CIO for that government entity. Not as large as the one in the south, but still in the top 50 US in terms of population.

The situation he walked into was similar to many of our CIO stories. The local government was very decentralized and had disparate systems that were not integrated. Many of the staff had been there a long time, appointed by favoritism rather than merit, and were reluctant to change. The previous administration had hired people to be CIOs who had no IT experience. He described it as the worst transition situation he had faced in his career. A group of executives loaned from industry had put together an assessment for the incoming administration which outlined most of the problems that he would face. IT savvy was low and there were very immature IT governance processes. The CIO recognized that informal leaders are crucial in government as the elected officials rarely get involved in the details. Working with two to three key people he developed relationships that led to better IT governance. He also rebuilt his IT leadership team including using two retired IT executives as part-time advisors. He relied on two key people on his team to teach him how the government actually worked.

Improving governance, project management and relationships has been successful. Attracting talent was a challenge due to compensation being below industry standards. After four years he moved back into the automotive industry as a CIO.

Leading IT in Higher Education

This CIO spent his entire career in higher education and is now retired. His niche was the Health Science or School of Medicine in each of three university where he worked as CIO. These schools consisted of academic, clinical and research units with multiple geographic branches. His role before retiring was to turnaround the organization of a large University Health Science system. This CIO joked that he should have asked more questions in the interview process!

The team that the CIO inherited was not strong. He made a lot of changes to the organization including laying people off. He made the point that you can actually remove people from higher education who are not performing. He focused on productivity and accountability. There was a sense of entitlement when he took over and he had to change that. One of the first application initiatives was a large ERP program. The mentality of the IT leadership was concern that if people were trained in the new system they would leave (which would result in untrained people staying)! By winnowing out people and bringing new people in, a new professionalism emerged in the IT organization, one that focused on customer service and delivering results on-time and budget.

The CIO created IT advisory groups comprised of executives from the lines of business (infrastructure, administration and research) in order to enhance governance. The university system raised $20+ million for IT infrastructure spending and all the line of business leaders were involved in prioritizing projects. This CIO went on to build a leadership development program for high potential IT professionals for a professional organization of medical schools.

The Stage Is Now Set…

In this chapter we discussed two dimensions of taking charge: the transition type and whether the CIO was an insider or an outsider. While there are four transition types, three characterize the most common, Turnaround,

Realignment and Success-Sustaining. Transition type matters to a newly appointed CIO because it describes the organizational situation in which the CIO finds themselves. It also indicates how much change the CIO will need to implement in taking charge of the role. While each type has unique challenges, these do not impact the taking charge process in terms of timeline or phases which are the two dimensions that we will discuss in the next chapter. We concluded with some "CIO stories" to give you a perspective on the CIOs that contributed to the project. Next, we will provide an overview of the taking charge process.

Notes

1. For a comprehensive discussion of leadership transitions see D. Ciampa and M. Watkins, *Right from the Start: Taking Charge in a New Leadership Role*, Harvard Business School Press, Boston, MA, 1999 and M. Watkins, *The First 90 Days: Proven Strategies for Getting up to Speed Faster and Smarter*, Harvard Business Review Press, Boston, 2013.
2. J.J. Gabarro, *The Dynamics of Taking Charge*, Harvard Business School Press, Boston, 1987.
3. J. Van Maanen and E.H. Schein, 'Toward a theory of organizational socialization', in: B.M. Shaw, ed., *Research in Organizational Behavior*, Greenwich, CT: JAI Press, 1979, pp. 209–264.
4. N. Fondas and M. Wiersema, 'Changing of the guard: The influence of CEO socialization on strategic change', *Journal of Management Studies*, Vol. 34, 1997, pp. 561–584 and R.R. Reilly, M.L. Tenopyr and S.M. Sperling, 'Effects of job previews on job acceptance and survival of telephone operator candidates', *Journal of Applied Psychology*, Vol. 64, No. 2, 1979, pp. 218–220.
5. See http://www.isaca.org/COBIT/Pages/COBIT-5.aspx, ISACA, Retrieved August 31, 2019, and https://www.axelos.com/best-practice-solutions/itil/what-is-itil

5

Beyond the First 90 Days: Taking Charge

In this chapter we present the generalized taking charge process for a newly appointed CIO that we have derived our data. As will be explained, this process consists of key activities and outcomes that occur across three overlapping, but distinct phases which follow a particular timeline. We will show how these activities relate to the transition types that were introduced in the previous chapter.

But before we describe the taking charge process, we want to address the question of whether the CIO faces challenges unique from other C-level executives. If not, then we would expect the taking charge process to be similar to other executives (in Chap. 3 we shared a few of those studies). If so, we would expect their taking charge process to be different because unique challenges would influence what is necessary to take charge effectively. If you have read this far you know that our position is that the CIO takes charge within a unique context. Others also share this view that CIO leadership is unique.[1] It is unique because the CIO (as we pointed out in Chap. 1) is expected to combine technical IT knowledge with an in-depth understanding of the organization across all functions, taking both an operational and strategic perspective, and where technology decisions can have a long-term implication. Moreover, unique leadership challenges arise from the technology/business interface, where active engagement and involvement of colleagues from outside the IT unit is mandatory for success as a CIO but so hard to accomplish.

© The Author(s) 2020
T. Gerth, J. Peppard, *Taking the Reins as CIO*,
https://doi.org/10.1007/978-3-030-31953-3_5

Why Is Taking Charge Different for CIOs?

While we agree with the distinctiveness of CIO leadership, we thought it would be interesting to ask non-IT executives the question. As we outlined in Chaps. 2 and 3, the CIO's success is dependent on many influences exerted by their non-IT executive peers, so their perspective matters. Our conversations with non-IT executives regarding the uniqueness of CIO leadership suggest the answer is both *yes* and *no*. Their perspective is valuable because it influences their expectations of a new CIO taking charge. When we asked them if a new CIO faces challenges unique from other executives when taking on a new appointment, they reported that many of the leadership challenges were similar. However, a number did surface some areas of uniqueness.

> I would think they [leadership challenges] are pretty similar…. I would think that their challenges are the same. Meaning, you've got to come in. You've got to build relationships. You've got to understand how the business operates. You've got to understand what the strengths and weaknesses are and the opportunities. You've got to have a good head about you to be able to prioritize and go after the biggest 'bang for the buck' and influence people. I think that no matter what, whether it's IT, Sales, or Marketing, I think it's very similar. V.P. Operations—Wire & Cable Manufacturer

> So, I don't think it's [unique], I mean I think the challenge for the [CIO] or the CTO is kind of similar to the CFO. Managing Director—Investment Bank

> I don't think so [are CIOs unique]. I would say they [CIO] have the same challenges as one of any of the staff positions. President—Regional Bank

Notice the final comment. Informed by his frame of reference (FoR), this bank president is clearly of the view that the CIO occupies a staff function, a point we will take up over the next few chapters.

Where executives recognized uniqueness was with the "context" of the CIO's taking charge. The following broad areas were mentioned:

- Being in a staff position versus operations (this was mentioned to be similar to engineering, HR, etc.).
- The reliance on influence to accomplish objectives.
- Role ambiguity in the sense that there were many expectations of CIOs and typically these were not completely understood or agreed across the organization.

- Technology was the most often cited challenge. The speed of technology change and keeping up with advances and how they can enable new opportunities.
- The necessity to have a strong understanding of all aspects of the organization.
- Leading a diverse talent pool with high market demand.

There were a group of executives that attributed unique challenges to any executive in a staff role rather than an operating leadership role.

That's [being a CIO is] a unique challenge … He has all the similar political issues, all the similar capital resource needs issues, all those things that any senior executive or leader has, but there's a technology component to it that the other people don't necessarily know. So that person has to have the ability to translate that. Chairman—Insurance Brokerage

No question. I mean, they're like any support organization, and the one that you really don't think about until you have a problem and then, all of a sudden, you're thinking about the guy running the IT organization, and it's usually negative. CEO—Diversified Manufacturer

CIO role ambiguity, highlighted in Chap. 1, was a consistent theme, highlighted as a significant challenge for CIOs.

The other difference, I think, is that you can go in an organization … almost always you walk into a situation where your peers get what you do and your role is accepted and understood, but for the CIO, it's often times not the case. I mean everybody kind of gets what the VP of Marketing and the VP of Sales and the VP of Manufacturing and so forth do. This comes back to the role understanding question that I've talked about and never really fixed. That's been around for a while I think, unfortunately. Regional V.P.—Mobile Telecommunication Operator

IT, often times, will be blamed for everything but the bad coffee and even they will be blamed for the bad coffee occasionally! So, it was really changing that; that mindset if you will. You know, I do think that they [challenges] are unique and that, historically, this is a new career and that it is seen as a high cost function with little clarity. So, suppose I am the new C.F.O; I think most people probably assume that when the new CFO walks in he knows what he is talking about and you see the CFO role more clearly. EVP & CFO—Power Utility

I think, in some respects, it is a bit of a thankless task by taking over any IT organization. I'm struggling to think of any IT organization, or I can think of very few, which are real world-class operations, recognized as being so by the peers and other people in the company. I don't think 'necessary evil' is the right phrase, but it's the best thing I can come up with. In the most part, it is being viewed as a necessary evil. I mean everybody notices when things don't go well, whether it's the e-mail system being down or whether there is some massive project failing. I think CIOs don't get huge amounts of credit normally when things go right, because people just expect it to go right. SVP & COO—Professional Services Firm

By far the most common set of comments from CxOs were regarding the unique challenges a CIO faces due to the rapid change and complexity of information technology. In the case of digital technologies, the velocity of change increases significantly.

I think it's a unique role. I can't think of any other disciplinary role that changes so fast from what's happening in the world. I mean technology itself is advancing, expanding and changing every single day. I don't think we can say that about Operations or Finance, but with technology in the world, for the IT leader, the unique thing is how do they stay on top of that and take what's happening around them and introduce this into an organization. And it is changing every single day. So, I think that's the unique thing about being an IT leader. In that regard, I'm glad I'm in Human Resources! V.P. Human Resources—Plastic & Rubber Manufacturer

I think they do [have unique challenges] because there is always a new 'leading edge' to what you are doing and if you picked Outlook over Lotus Notes 20 years ago, you got it right. And then a lot of executives don't face those types of challenges, or at least not some that are measured in such open referendums that everyone can see, so I think that some of the challenges are unique. Managing Director—Investment Bank

I think that from an IT perspective it is untenable the amount of information and new technologies that are on the market and to be able to discern is this business value add; what business problem is this going to solve? The velocity and volume of new technology is just, like I said, untenable. And the biggest challenge is, what do I bring to the table and how do I know it's going to work. V.P. Supply Chain—Logistics Services Company

CIOs face many of the same leadership challenges as other executives when they take charge. We did not expect anything different and our conversations with non-IT executives bore that out. However, this similarity ends with the CIO's unique contextual challenges (as described in Chap. 2). These unique challenges yielded a process of taking charge for the CIO that is different from other executives and a newly appointed CIO needs to consider this when they begin their transition.

The Taking Charge Process

Taking charge is a process. It is a process that consists of activities, relationships between the activities and a timeline of execution of those activities. We found that CIOs take charge in three distinct and overlapping phases that happen across a particular timeline. Moreover, our research has shown that to take charge requires two to three years. A prescient comment that we continually heard was captured by one CIO we spoke to: *"Don't drink the Kool-Aid and believe you can be successful as a CIO by reading the 90-day plan checklist in a book somewhere!"* In the rest of this chapter we will present an overview of this process, with a deeper dive into each of the phases in the following chapter.

In our interviews with CIOs, they described to us both the timeline of their taking charge process as well as the types of activities in which they engaged. Based on this data, we identified phases based on common themes from their descriptions of what they told us they did when they were transitioning, the outcomes they achieved, the problems they experienced, the timeframes in which they occurred and the lessons they learned. We labeled these phases Entry, Stabilization and Renewal. Entry focuses on learning the organization's issues and strengths and establishing confidence. Stabilization is the phase where CIOs built credibility as the IT leader. The renewal phase is where the CIO transitions from simply being the IT leader to become a legitimate business leader. In essence, CIOs experience the taking charge process in three overlapping phases that lead to building confidence, credibility and legitimacy over time.

CIOs always experience an Entry phase upon initial transition into the role. This is the same for insiders (internal promotions) as well as outsiders (external hires). The Stabilization phase begins shortly after the new CIO starts (although it could start immediately in an extreme turnaround transition) and lasts approximately 9–12 months. The Renewal phase starts approximately six months into an appointment and overlaps the Stabilization phase. These phases and the taking charge timeline are shown below in Fig. 5.1.

The Entry phase consists of two activities that can be described as learning and diagnosis. All the CIOs described a learning process of getting to know

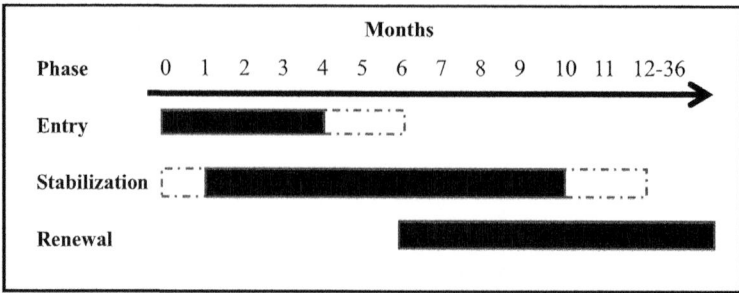

Fig. 5.1 Taking charge phases over time. (Source: Based on A.B. Gerth and J. Peppard, 'How newly appointed CIOs take charge', *MIS Quarterly Executive*, Vol. 13, No. 3, pp. 159–173)

the business of the organization and the objectives of its executive leadership team. CIOs also use this time to diagnose the IT-related problems in the organization. The outcome of this Entry phase is a working knowledge of the organization for the new CIO. This working knowledge consists of who the key players are, their objectives and what "keeps them up at night". It also provides the CIO with an assessment of their IT leadership team and the efficacy of IT governance in the organization. The politics and the organization's culture are also critical areas about which CIOs attempt to make sense of. The entry process typically lasts anywhere from four to six months and sets the stage for Stabilization and Renewal phases.

The Stabilization phase begins shortly after the CIO starts in the position and lasts for approximately 9–12 months. This phase consists of three sets of activities: taking corrective action and delivering existing projects, building the IT leadership team and designing and implementing basic IT governance processes. There are several key outcomes of this phase. One is that the CIO gains credibility through effective delivery of IT services and projects. The other key outcomes are that the CIO builds their own IT leadership team and implements basic mechanisms to govern IT. Implementing fundamental IT governance processes sets boundaries with CxO peers with regards to IT investment decisions and prioritization. By building their own leadership team the CIO creates a group of leaders who buy into their vision and are capable of delivering strategic initiatives to the business.

The CIO now has gained credibility as an IT leader, has governance processes to determine IT spend and prioritize IT initiatives with significant business impact and a leadership team in place to execute those initiatives. This dynamic of building credibility through performance in the role is consistent with research in role theory as well as leader socialization introduced in Chap. 3.[2]

The Renewal phase is characterized by the CIO building on their credibility to implement changes that position them to become a legitimate business leader. In this phase they focus on contributing more to the strategic direction of the organization. Renewal normally starts in months 12–18 and continues the work begun in the Stabilization phase to enhance the IT leadership team and the organization's IT governance processes. CIOs focus on increasing business knowledge in their IT teams as well as the IT knowledge of their business colleagues. They exert influence in setting IT strategy and being viewed as a business leader rather than simply the leader of an IT unit. The overall taking charge process is summarized in Table 5.1 below.

We were curious about whether these phases might change depending on the transition type. This analysis revealed patterns that enabled us to develop descriptions of the phases across the transition types. What was apparent from the data was that for each transition type, CIOs implemented degrees of change ranging from significant to incremental. As might be expected, Turnaround and Realignment transition types demanded significant changes, while Success-Sustaining transitions required the least.

While transition type did not influence the number of phases or the key activities, diving a little deeper there was some variance in the degree of change and effort required in each phase, depending on the transition type. The following is a discussion of how the activities of each phase vary by transition type. We do not propose to prescribe a specific playbook for every transition that a CIO might face. However, we can share observations of how each taking charge phase is influenced by the transition type in which it occurs.

Table 5.1 CIO taking charge phases, activities and outcomes

Phase/ timeframe	Entry (Month 0–6)	Stabilization (Month 1–12)	Renewal (Month 6–24+)
Key activities	Learning about the organization Diagnosing service delivery issues Building relationships Assessing personnel Evaluating IT governance	Improving service Delivering in-flight projects Building IT leadership team Implementing IT governance	Influencing strategic initiatives Enhancing the IT team Building IT savvy of senior leadership team
Outcomes	Confidence Understanding of issues Action agenda	Credibility as IT leader Influence via IT leaders Control via governance	Legitimacy as business leader Increased IT strategic contribution Improved senior leadership team IT savvy

Source: Based on A.B. Gerth and J. Peppard, 'How newly appointed CIOs take charge', *MIS Quarterly Executive*, Vol. 13, No. 3, pp. 159–173

Start-Up Transitions

Start-up transitions are when CIO is charged with assembling the capabilities (people, funding, information and technology) to get a new business off the ground. Start-up transitions provide the CIO with a lot of discretion about how they develop the role. In fact, often with Start-ups there is no CIO at all, but rather a Chief Technology Officer (CTO). Typically, start-up organizations are technology oriented and the initial activities are more focused on the product technology rather than the organization's IT infrastructure. As the start-up matures, the need for a CIO business leader becomes more important. The activities in taking charge are not as intense as Turnaround and Realignment transitions, but time is of the essence.

Entry

There is always an Entry phase because there is always a first 90–100 days in any transition! However, Start-up transitions imply that the business has just been established and the objectives and culture and politics are evolving as well. Depending on when the CIO actually comes on-board and whether he/she has a prior relationship to the CEO and other executives or the founders really dictates the amount of learning that will take place. Often a CIO will take a role in a start-up when he/she does not have a relationship with the entire leadership team and therefore there will be more learning required in that situation.

Stabilization

For the start-up CIO, the Stabilization phase of taking charge is always about getting things up and running. The CIO must build the IT leadership team from scratch which usually take priority starting in the Entry phase and continuing into the Stabilization phase. Projects must be initiated that build the organization's technology infrastructure for front-office and back-office operations. Applications may also be needed to provide competitive advantage, depending on the business model of the start-up. This is a broad generalization of course, as start-ups are all different and require different levels of technology support. Suffice it to say the start-up CIO is very busy in this phase! IT governance is important, but since the management team might be relatively small, complex processes are likely not needed at this point. This does not imply that IT governance can be ignored but at least some simple IT governance should to be put into place.

Renewal

The Renewal phase does allow the CIO the opportunity to evolve from the back-office technology supplier to a more strategic member of the management team. This might even happen sooner than other transition types because of the rapid growth of the company. In this phase, the CIO can build upon what they initiated in the stabilization phase to enhance their team, modify governance as needed and influence the strategic direction of the organization.

Start-up transitions really allow a CIO to put their stamp on the organization quickly and build a leadership team and governance processes from scratch. CIOs have a lot of discretion in this type of transition, but there is also a need for speed when providing the technology foundation of a new business.

Turnaround Transitions

In a Turnaround transition, the newly appointed CIO takes on an IT organization that is "in trouble" and works to get it back on track. In this transition context, the perception of the top leadership team is that information and technology is not delivering expected business outcomes, and the previous CIO was seen as having failed to meet expectations. This transition type is often a result of a change-over in the CEO role and/or a change in strategic direction. Unlike the start-up, the CIO inherits a complex set of expectations, technology, leadership resources among other things.

Entry

With this transition, the CIO's time for learning is significantly curtailed as the focus is on having an immediate impact. CIOs emphasize achieving short-term priorities of colleagues. Their working assumption is that IT governance is immature and key IT personnel will need to be replaced. While they have less time to focus on relationship building per se, getting things done helps build confidence in the CIO as an impactful leader.

Stabilization

The urgency of the situation can require radical changes to be made almost immediately on taking up the role, often without complete knowledge of the issues. The CIO will probably spend significant time on tactical "firefighting" and dealing with operational problems and issues around service and project delivery and customer engagement. The priority is to immediately assess the project portfolio to assess viability and overall business contribution. Outsourcing contracts, if they exist, are usually renegotiated to reflect requirements for turnaround. Turnaround CIOs typically make radical changes to the IT organization and key personnel are replaced. IT governance changes are often limited initially to project governance but will need to extend to prioritization of spend on technology. The focus is on (re)building the reputation of IT organization.

Renewal

Turnaround CIOs usually take longer than other transition types to enter this phase. Turnarounds require more significant effort and time in the Stabilization phase to sort out in-flight projects, improve service levels and build the leadership team and therefore delay the transition to Renewal. Significant effort is made to increase C-suite IT savvy through demonstrated delivery of value. Depending on the situation inherited, having strategic influence can extend well into year 2 and beyond. However, Turnaround CIOs often enjoy a high degree of credibility and legitimacy after accomplishing a tough assignment in the Stabilization phase. This sets them up well to make more strategic impact in the Renewal phase.

Realignment Transitions

The new CIO is hired to revitalize an IT organization that is "drifting into trouble". Prior to the CIO's appointment, tensions were beginning to emerge, often due to a new reporting line for the CIO, changes in the makeup of the IT leadership team or a new mandate for IT (e.g. a shift from cost minimization to a more strategic role). Given the new expectations, the existing IT organization was often characterized as "not fit for purpose", but not necessarily in trouble.

Entry

On taking up the role, the new CIO usually has a good steer from the recruitment process that some realignment is required. Usually the executive leadership team is open to engaging with the CIO, but he/she has to be proactive. Review of IT organization structure, role and personnel is part of this phase like any transition. This assessment will result in recognition that some aspects of IT are effective while others are not. From this, the CIO should be able to identify an effective "go-forward" plan of action.

Stabilization

IT project and service portfolios are assessed to determine the extent of misalignment and corrective action is taken. Incremental changes are made to the IT leadership team which may include some replacements or re-deployment. IT governance structure, processes and mechanisms are updated to correct any misalignment. Outsourcing contracts are often renegotiated to reflect new requirements and visions of the relationship.

Renewal

Correction of any misalignment with business objectives generates openness within the top leadership team for the CIO to begin to engage in a strategic dialogue. With this transition type, CIOs reported that their CxO peers requested that they be more strategic rather than just operationally focused. Therefore, the move from stabilization to renewal was easier for Realignment CIOs than for Turnaround CIOs.

Realignment transitions offer a great opportunity for a CIO. The realignment is normally aimed at increasing the strategic contribution of information and technology and therefore increasing the influence of the CIO. Realignments imply that while there is satisfaction with IT, some adjustments are necessary. Improvement opportunities are often well known and stakeholders are usually willing to engage.

Success-Sustaining Transitions

The Success-sustaining transition is perhaps the "easiest" of the four types. The new CIO takes responsibility to preserve the vitality of a successful IT organization but also to "take it to the next level". The previous CIO is perceived as being successful and having performed well in the role and has either moved into a new role, to a new organization or retired.

Entry

The CIO has a reasonable time to learn about the organization and assess current situation before making any changes. Key emphasis is to build relationships and understand priorities. The plan of action is normally to move IT to "the next level" rather than any significant corrections.

Stabilization

Incremental changes may be made to the IT leadership team. If necessary, IT governance structure, processes and mechanisms are updated to revitalize business engagement in core decision areas. However, the CIO must ensure that the organization doesn't become complacent. In this phase the CIO must at least preserve existing performance and avoid any degradation in service.

Renewal

Because IT is perceived as being successful, this phase is entered much earlier than other transition types. Emphasis is placed on achieving greater strategic influence for IT and maintaining the positive trajectory of the IT organization.

As long as the shared understanding of success exists, the new CIO's role initially is "if it's not broken, don't fix it". No executive wants to be known as the one who ruined a successful organization! Gradually, the CIO can put her/his own stamp on the organization as they build credibility and legitimacy in the same manner as CIOs do in other transition types.

Taking Charge

While executives' perspectives on the nature of the CIO leadership challenges vary, our research suggests that the taking charge process for newly appointed CIOs is unique compared to other executives. Challenges that are specific to a CIO include the ambiguity of the role, the enterprise breadth of the role, leading a continuum of professionals from the highly technical to the more business-oriented as well as the rapid pace of change in technology and getting active involvement and engagement from colleagues outside of the IT unit. All of these factors influence the timeframes, phases, activities and key outcomes that we have outlined in this chapter. The intersection of transition type and the taking charge process highlights some important variations within the process in terms of urgency and intensity of required changes. In the following chapter we will dive deeper into each taking charge phase and hear from CIOs what their experience has been.

Notes

1. See, for example, E. Karahanna and R. Watson, 'Information systems leadership', *IEEE Transactions on Engineering Management,* Vol. 53, 2006, pp. 171–176; C. Ranganathan and S. Jha, 'Do CIOs matter? Assessing the value of CIO presence in top management teams', in *Proceedings of the International Conference on Information Systems*, Association of Information Systems, 2008, Paris and J. Peppard, 'The conundrum of IT management', *European Journal of Information Systems*, Vol. 16, 2007, pp. 336–345.
2. For examples see D. Katz and R. L. Kahn, *The Social Psychology of Organizations*, New York, Wiley, 1978 and J.L. Denis, A. Langley and M. Pineault, 'Becoming a leader in a complex organization', *Journal of Management Studies,* Vol. 37, 2000, pp. 1063–1100.

6

The Phases of Taking Charge

In this chapter, we want to dive into the details of each of the taking charge phases. There is a lot of information to unpack regarding what happens in each phase, key areas of focus and the outcomes that result. The flow of the chapter is to discuss each phase and highlight where our analysis indicates CIOs should focus and to provide illustrations of what they told us they did to be effective in doing what they deemed necessary. Some areas for attention are unique to a phase, while others form a thread throughout all three phases. For example, learning and assessment primarily occurs in the entry phase. While activities in focal areas such as the IT leadership team, peer IT savvy, IT governance and building relationships occur across phases, they become more emphasized as time progresses.

We share many quotes from the CIOs we have spoken to in order to bring their insights and experiences about taking charge to life. What was interesting for us was that they share many common experiences even though every transition is unique. This enabled us to see patterns and threads which ultimately lead to delineate the three phases and the content of each phase.

The Entry Phase

The entry phase is the first phase of taking charge and consists of variety of activities that can be summed up as learning and diagnosis. All CIOs described a learning process of getting to know the business of the organization (its strategy, customers and competitive dynamics), the objectives and priorities

© The Author(s) 2020
T. Gerth, J. Peppard, *Taking the Reins as CIO*,
https://doi.org/10.1007/978-3-030-31953-3_6

of each executive team member and to understand their expectations. They also used the early weeks and months to diagnose IT-related problems.

Several mechanisms were used by CIOs during the entry process to accomplish learning and diagnosis. The most frequently used was interviewing, having one-on-one discussions with non-IT stakeholders and IT leaders alike to help them build a comprehensive picture of the situation they now found themselves in. Another mechanism was observation, whereby they watched how decisions were made and how people behaved, particularly during meetings. Lastly, they reviewed existing documentation such as budgets, status reports and plans. This "tour" of the organization and key stakeholders is described by CIOs in a similar way.

> The first 60 days was 7am to 7pm every single day, six, sometimes seven days per week. At the end of 60 days I remember distinctly waking up one morning and thinking I finally get it. I understand where all the skeletons are. I understand who all the people are. I understand all the processes. I understand what the priorities are; now let's go make some changes! CIO—Semi-conductor Manufacturer

> The first thing I did in the first 90 days was sit down with every functional department leader. This not only helped me learn the business, but also to build critical relationships. I asked, 'what are your biggest problems right now'? CIO—Air Ambulance Service

> I would say that the first three to four months I didn't change much. I certainly established a 90-day plan that consisted of meeting with the organization (leaders), assessing talent, and things like that. CIO—Professional Services Firm

> The 90-day diagnostic was … spending time with people and asking what they viewed as the issues and opportunities. I also visited a number of the properties. CIO—Hospitality Organization

> I went out and met with every VP and we had management meetings, so we were a tight-knit group. CIO—Hand Tool Manufacturer

Some CIOs also made the point that they sought input from the direct reports of their c-suite peers, taking them closer to the stakeholders that actually used the technology services and solutions and worked with staff from the IT unit. This approach took the CIOs deeper into the user organization.

> In not all cases did I go to the leader of that functional area, but to the people who actually used the application. CIO—Air Ambulance Service

> I met with the department leaders and also their direct reports one-on-one to understand their issues and priorities. CIO—Municipal Government

The concept of the first 90–100 days was commonly mentioned by CIOs. However, this period was not the timeframe it took to take charge, rather, CIO reported that it took between four and six months before they felt they had enough of an understanding of the organization's issues and people and could begin making significant decisions.

> Four, maybe 6 months into it … I think you begin to gain … technical and organizational confidence. CIO—Semi-conductor Manufacturer

> The first six months were really just learning the job. I think … 4–6 months is the period for you to get your bearings, know who's who, who's on first. You feel like you can make some really strong decisions after that period. So, I would say that after 4–6 months I was feeling that. CIO—Federal Regulatory Agency

> It is really 4–6 months before you get your bearings, know who's who and feel like you can make some really strong decisions. CIO—Professional Services Firm

> Within 6 months I had confidence I understood the situation. CIO—Hospitality Organization

> If you are coming into a company as a brand new CIO, you need to assess for 3–6 months what needs to go on … within 6 months my confidence was building. CIO—Hand Tool Manufacturer

The more experienced CIOs advised pushing out as far as possible any decisions that would result in having to make changes, particularly those likely to cause significant ripples cross the organization. They emphasized the importance of learning and diagnosing the situation in which they found themselves. They acknowledged that there is a danger, even temptation, to begin instigating changes quickly as it is only natural to want to lay down your intent. While going for the quick win might seem logical, the advice is to resist; the "quick wins paradox" has been written about.[1] What is important to determine is the pace of change that the organization is capable of absorbing.

> So, what we've introduced … we spent a lot of time introducing, carefully introducing and the phrase we use … introducing things at a culturally appropriate speed. CIO—Semi-conductor Manufacturer

> If you are a sprinter and you come into a walking organization you are going to walk. I actually had to slow down a little bit on some things and conclude you can only do one large change at a time. One thing I am always wary of when you come into a place requiring a lot of change is … change fatigue. CIO—Insurance Provider

> It always amazes me how hard it is and how slow it is to drive change. CIO—Pharmaceutical Manufacturer

CIOs should also strive to understand the culture of the organization and the change capacity that exists. This is not to inhibit introducing change but rather moderate the speed and degree of change that can be introduced. Culture can sometimes be a double-edged sword, and the CIO of an apparel retailer gave us a good example of this.

> The culture of [company] is very community minded—it is the nicest retail culture I have ever experienced. That's quite wonderful but it's also—it's very much accepted mediocrity and kind of our best days have already happened which is … not part of the culture that you would want to have in a growing business with lots of disrupters. So, my boss and I spent a lot of time talking about how do we sharpen the elbows on this culture but not lose some of the really wonderful parts of the culture.

The three areas in particular that receive most attention during this phase are the IT leadership team, IT governance processes and the IT savvy of their top management team peers.

IT Leadership Team Assessment

One area of assessment by CIOs was the state of their IT leadership team. A strong leadership team is viewed as critical to success:

> [Your IT leadership team] is crucial, absolutely crucial. You cannot do every project yourself. We've got an investment portfolio of $110 million. If I don't have people who really know their stuff and can build their own relationships with the business [partners] then we're going nowhere. CIO—Consumer Products Manufacturer

> You want to hire the best of the best; you want to have people that you trust that can really have your back. CIO—Federal Regulatory Agency

> I suppose in the first three months I tried to identify the key people who were the keepers and we couldn't do without. CIO—Gaming Industry

Most of the CIOs we spoke to assessed the IT leadership team they inherited in need of some rebuilding. However, the extent of that rebuilding was dependent on the type of transition they faced. Some expressed serious reservations about their team and felt it did not meet the profile expected in a modern digital enterprise.

They were viewing themselves as IT leaders where, I think, senior IT folks at that level really need to view themselves as business leaders. CIO—Electronics Distribution Company

The biggest surprise was … the fundamental lack of competence of the existing staff. It was a big, happy, dysfunctional family, with the blind leading the blind. CIO—Engineering Software Firm

[W]e had a lot of deep technologists without much business acumen or a sense of aligning the work they were doing with providing value to the business. CIO—Professional Services Firm

I would say we had relatively weak players relative to the challenges we were facing. CIO—Hospitality Organization

As might be expected, IT leadership teams were seldom faulted for having inadequate technical skills. The capabilities most often cited as lacking were project management competence, a lack of business acumen (including understanding the business of the organization that employed them) and poor communication skills. The capability of the IT leadership was not always criticized as individual personal failings, rather as a symptom of the previous leader's view of IT and how it should be resourced and organized.

In most cases, CIOs in Turnaround or Realignment transitions were working for a CEO who had been recently hired, with the CIO's appointment the result of changes that he/she was making as part of their own taking-change process. This new CEO had a different set of expectations for IT than his/her predecessor. This was usually that information and technology must contribute more to operational and strategic performance as he/she looked to move information and technology center stage. CIOs explained that a lack of attention and investment in technology and talent had rendered the function incapable of meeting this new mandate.

Some of the people still working for me got a bad rap from their stakeholders. But they were set up to fail. CIO—Consumer Products Manufacturer

During the downturn, they [previous top management and CIO] made a fiscal decision to release the majority of senior people to reduce payroll. They took out all the people with experience. So, there were substantial morale problems. CIO—Computer Manufacturer

The CIO of a semi-conductor manufacturer in Silicon Valley recounted that everyone in the CIO community were familiar with the challenges of the company he was interviewing with, through all the various contacts … I knew what the situation was like over there. The CIO reported to the CFO and it was being treated as a cost center … so the situation with the IT leadership was troubled.

Recognizing that the IT leadership team requires some rebuilding leads to actions been taken during the stabilization phase. Of course, every team is unique and the challenge for the CIO is to objectively assess the team's individual strengths and weaknesses and determine how to build a team that could meet his/her expectations and, by implications, those of the C-suite.

IT Governance Process Maturity

CIOs described different maturity levels for the type of governance around IT they inherited. These depended greatly on the transition type. For Turnaround situations, comments from CIOs like "non-existent", "low" or "not very mature" were common. Somewhat surprisingly, the specific term "non-existent" came up more often than expected.

> There weren't any. There really were no financial governance nor operational governance processes in place. CIO—Computer Manufacturer

> They were simply non-existent. CIO—Insurance Company

> The IT governance processes were, they were really non-existent. CIO—Hospitality Organization

Not all the CIOs that reported low IT governance maturity used such an extreme description. More often, they simply described governance maturity as low or informal when they arrived. This was particularly for Realignment transitions and indicated an improvement opportunity.

> It was pretty informal. We have regional business units and that's where the budget power is. When I came in, the 7 regional presidents were the governance. CIO—Electronics Distributor

> I would say that IT governance was pretty immature. We probably had some alignment with individual stakeholders … I'm not sure we ever looked across those and said here's our corporate priority … our strategic direction. CIO—Professional Services Firm

> [T]hat we had to have processes and portfolio boards at whatever level was kind of understood, however poorly or well they operated at the time. So, we took the opportunity to refresh. CIO—Consumer Products Manufacturer

Frequently, we heard stories where there were particular IT governance mechanisms in place, but not adhered to. This, in itself, was a signal to the incoming CIO of the challenges that would likely be encountered.

> They were pretty non-existent. There were some processes in place, but having a process and actually following it are two different things. CIO—Gaming Company

Where CIOs reported IT governance requiring little if any attention, these were primarily in Realignment and especially Success-sustaining transitions.[2] As the CIO of a Federal Regulatory Agency noted to us regarding IT governance at the agency when he took over:

> Yeah, it was [mature] … there was already a group that had been established to help make governance decisions much like a CIO council if you will. It was actually more of an IT council. But we met regularly and routinely discuss major issues, such things as like the digital platform, security, enterprise architecture. CIO—Federal Regulatory Agency

While IT governance processes were assessed during the Entry phase, implementing improved IT governance processes emerged as a priority during the Stabilization phase when they were considered as immature.

CxO IT Savvy

IT savvy was described by CIOs as how well the top executives of the organization understand and appreciate the role that information and technology can play in helping them meet their business objectives. This relates to the broader frame of reference (FoR) concept that we outlined in Chap. 2. It is a recognition of how IT can impact performance, both operationally and strategically. In addition, it is about understanding how information and technology generate business value and what the role of non-IT executive is in that quest. It does not mean that non-IT executives are deeply knowledgeable about information technology itself. In the following paragraphs, we present what we found when we scratched beneath the surface of this understanding to examine their FoR.

In the Entry phase, the CIOs assess how well their c-suite peers recognized the contribution of information and technology to the business. Often the level of IT savvy among the top management teams was described as low. Comments such as these illustrate the challenge that some CIOs faced:

Very, very low. CIO—Computer Manufacturer

Zero. It's not negative, but it's zero. CIO—Petroleum Refining Company

Pretty un-savvy I would say. CIO—Gaming Company

While this is a generalization, there were individual exceptions within senior executive teams. In general, low IT savvy assessments were the rule for CIOs in Turnaround transitions and common in Realignment transitions.

CIOs, particularly in technology-oriented service firms, reported that their top managers were relatively savvy about how technology could be used strategically as it was the core of their services business. This assessment tended to be in Success-sustaining transitions and occasionally in Realignment transitions. Some examples where executives were cited for their IT savvy:

Pretty savvy actually. They know what technology can be applied to business advantage. CIO—Electronics Distributor

'The COO' knows that [the company] is really an information management company and information technology is critical. CIO—Insurance Company

I mean most of our leaders come from professional services firms and are very IT savvy. CIO—IT Services Firm

There is the guy who is Managing Director for the on-line business and he is pretty IT savvy. CIO—Gaming Company

While individual executives may have displayed varying levels of IT savvy, often the CIOs felt that their overall IT savvy as a group was low, as their predecessor had not demonstrated they could add value. This was consistent with some of the earlier comments about the existing IT leadership team; no CIO we spoke to actually blamed low IT savvy on the executive team, but rather on the IT leader. CIOs felt it was their responsibility to develop the FoR of their top executive peers regarding information and technology. Some of the comments from them that capture this sentiment include:

I think because of the former situation they just viewed IT as the people around the networks and those that tried to keep the servers running. CIO—Semiconductor Manufacturer

I think the business' perspective of IT was as a service provider and not how IT could be an asset to the business. CIO—Professional Services Firm

When IT savvy is assess as in need of overhaul, increasing the CxOs' understanding of the potential contribution by IT becomes a priority during the Renewal phase.

The outcome of the entry phase is a working knowledge of the organization for the new CIO. This working knowledge consists of who the key players are, their objectives and what "keeps them up at night," as well as the culture and politics of the organization. It also provides the CIO with an assessment of their IT leadership team, the efficacy of IT governance in the organization and some sense of the FoR of the individual c-suite members.

The Stabilization Phase

The second phase of taking charge is the Stabilization phase. This phase begins shortly after the CIO joins the organization and lasts for approximately 9–12 months. The Stabilization phase consists of three major sets of activities: taking corrective action for service delivery and delivering existing projects, building the IT leadership team and implementing basic IT governance processes.

As a new CIO you must build credibility with your new executive peers that you can take care of your "own house" and effectively run the IT organization. In Turnaround and Realignment transitions, this is critically important because service and project delivery failures typically contributed to the previous CIO's exit from the organization.

Service/Project Delivery

Taking corrective action is based on the CIO's diagnosis of services that require improvement. These problems are identified by speaking to stakeholders during the initial months of the entry phase and through the CIO's own observation as well as based on their experience in previous organizations.

> I came in the first month and said we're going to have a single directory in 60 days and at the end of 60 days we had one directory in place. The feedback was overwhelmingly positive. CIO—Computer Manufacturer

> [T]he interesting thing about establishing credibility was that I got concussions from all the low hanging fruit. I went to every department and said give me your top 5 client problems. Then we went out and actively attacked the number 1 pain point in every department … then they say 'hey you got this done in 7 days and your predecessor couldn't get it done in 1 ½ years!'. CIO—Insurance Company

I had an understanding with my boss on priorities and the first 60 days it was highly reactive, just break-fix. In IT there were some areas that definitely needed some assistance. The CEO called me and said, well, your first assignment is you got to fix our helpless desk. CIO—Hand Tool Manufacturer

Improving IT services is not the only priority. The incoming CIO also needs to deliver IT projects deemed critical that are already in-flight when they arrive. Doing both is a way to build credibility.

You need to focus on building credibility through delivery. CIO—Consumer Products Manufacturer

I determined with the President what the priorities were in terms of immediate deliverables. Being a private company, there were some [previous] transformational promises made and it was my job to execute and deliver on those. CIO—Hospitality Organization

You know to make sure you can get in front of them [non-IT business partners] and they say, 'I can rely on IT to respond and add value.' CIO—Professional Services Firm

An Insider CIO remarked:

I had kicked off several major projects within two weeks…, but I already knew what needed to be done. I think that is an unfair advantage compared to somebody from the outside in terms of how fast they can get things done. CIO—Hand Tool Manufacturer

The credibility earned in this phase provides CIOs the platform to make more strategic changes (which occur in the Renewal phase).

One of our fundamental approaches was executing on [current project] in order to realize the expected savings and credibility. [This resulted in] an accelerated investment in IT that the company required because of the pent-up demand for IT services. CIO—Hospitality Organization

Ask for the pain and listen. Never, never, never promise something you do not already know you can deliver. CIO—Insurance Company

The CIO of a global consumer goods manufacturing company explained building credibility with his executive peers in Customer Development this way:

You don't get to talk to these guys [the Customer Development executives] unless you understand your own world. So, I need to understand all of the Customer

Development systems that support them. I need to know what is working and what is not working. What investments in IT have they made that get a good ROI and those that do not. The reason is quite simple, if I can convince them that I know what technology is supporting their world, then that gets me partially through the door with them. I can use that knowledge to advise them of where they should put their money or where they should focus resources. That's the real 'pay-off'. It's all about building trust and credibility, mostly credibility through delivery.

Solving IT service problems and delivering existing projects are two ways that CIOs take action during the stabilization phase. The stabilization phase involves making immediate changes to IT services that stakeholders identify as broken and that the CIO can impact in a short time. This brings quick benefits for the organization, but it primarily provides credibility to the new CIO. The outcome is that the CIO is seen by his/her peers as a credible functional leader and someone they can trust to delivery what is promised.

Building the IT Leadership Team

One of the first actions any incoming CIO takes is to communicate with their team his/her expectations and to begin the process of building trust. The importance of the IT leadership team to the success of the CIO was widely recognized by all the CIOs we spoke to.[3] A strong IT leadership team is required in order to effectively collaborate with colleague from the business side as well as deliver key IT initiatives that create business value.

The CIO of a large Federal agency and a veteran of several Federal CIO posts noted to us:

> You want to hire the best, you want people you can trust and that really have your back. You want a deputy in place that will complement your strengths.

The second major area of action in the Stabilization phase is to assess and refresh, as necessary, members of the team reporting to the CIO. Many of the CIOs in our research started by lifting the morale of their existing team. Particularly in Turnaround and Realignment transitions, the business partners' perception of the IT organization was often negative and of course, this impacted the team's self-image.

> One of the things that was important to me for my team was to first build their reputation as being the most transparent, the most critical judge of our own performance. That takes a little time to build-up that kind of reputation. CIO—Electronics Distribution

The CIO of a semiconductor manufacturer and a veteran Silicon Valley executive described the scenario he inherited during a turnaround as follows:

> The IT leadership team was pretty down-trodden. They didn't see any light at the end of the tunnel until I arranged to report to the CEO, which gave them some hope. There was still a lot of skepticism that the CEO would really give IT the time, latitude and resources we needed. In the first 9 months we added a significant number of new people and a lot of dollars to IT, so I think people are beginning to see that the Titanic is turning! The business realized that they had under-invested in IT and perhaps now was the right time to invest … more in the people and technology for the growth that is expected. I saw a lot of opportunity to work with both the executive team and the IT organization to lay out a plan for what we had to do as well as the required commitments. I think we've been able to establish a lot of credibility with both the IT folks as well as the executive staff.

CIOs establish themselves as the leaders of their teams, but also worked to build positive relationships as described by this CIO:

> I asked for their input as opposed to excluding them. When I made a decision that was contrary to the way it had been done in the past, I helped them understand why and what my rationale was for that. We established good rapport up front and I was very clear about what my intentions were. So that, in my mind, is very important because if your staff don't believe in you or trust you, I don't know that you can be successful. CIO—Air Ambulance Service

Although building trust and a rapport with the IT leadership team is one action that CIOs take during Stabilization, significant changes in personnel may also be required. CIOs in Turnaround transitions reported replacing a high percentage of their leadership teams during this phase.

> I've spent a lot of my time the last year restructuring my team, hiring new people and getting new senior leadership in technology. CIO—Computer Manufacturer

> In the last two and half years I have replaced all of the people who reported to me when I walked in the door. I have elevated some talent and brought some talent in from outside. It's been a very gradual and deliberate shift in the overall mix of team … and it's dramatically strengthened. CIO—Hospitality Organization

Often CIOs brought in leaders that they had worked with in the past and brought with them that trusted relationship. Teams were built by drawing on the professional network of the CIO.

I replaced 70% of the management team and that's primarily because those folks were promoted up from individual contributor roles from very low levels due to no fault of their own. There were some folks that I knew from the past and I reached out after my first month and created roles. We brought them into my organization in the third month. CIO—Computer Manufacturer

I've been fortunate because I've actually had a very strong IT team and some of them have followed me from other jobs. CIO—Petroleum Refining Company

I did actually bring in two people that I had worked with before. CIO—Professional Services Firm

Rebuilding the IT leadership team in terms of reputation and capability is a priority of CIOs in the Stabilization phase of taking charge. Replacing some incumbents with people viewed as more capable by the CIO contribute to building credibility with non-IT business partners and builds the foundation for executing strategic initiatives. A high performing team also consolidates the CIO's power base with trustworthy leaders.

Implementing IT Governance

As we have indicated during our description of the Entry phase, an overwhelming majority of the CIOs we spoke to identified significant improvement opportunities in their IT governance processes. Designing and implementing new IT governance processes and mechanisms is a common task during Stabilization.

One of the first things we did actually was put a more collaborative IT governance process in place. Select those guys in charge but expose them to more of the varying demands of what they need to invest in IT and also we made things much more transparent in terms of reporting progress. CIO—Electronics Distributor

We are introducing … IT governance processes, we don't really call them that here, including a kind of IT steering committee, for lack of a better description, with the senior executives. We've got a full program management office now. We have certified program managers in place. We've got a lot of work going on around COBIT and ITIL and what we found to be the most useful, again because of their lack of knowledge around these frameworks, is to change some of the wording, not to make it sound so process heavy, I think people see value in having a conversation around processes and controls even if we don't really call it processes. CIO—Semi-conductor Manufacturer

We had to put in place a change management process. We had to put in place an IT steering committee. CIO—Air Ambulance Service

We established a quarterly IT operating review with metrics around each of the key areas of service delivery. CIO—Hospitality Organization

CIOs initiate or enhance IT governance processes to achieve two objectives. The first is to take control over IT operations such as infrastructure and applications. This consists of stopping ad hoc decision-making regarding technology purchases as well as implementing technology standards to guide a more formal decision-making process. The CIO exerts more control over IT operations in order to fix and improve service delivery issues identified in the Entry phase. The second is to define decision rights regarding future IT investment decisions and prioritization. Both of these objectives establish the CIO's authority to control IT operations and to facilitate more formality and transparency in decision-making within the executive leadership team regarding IT investments. Improving IT governance and demonstrating its impact is another way for the CIO to establish legitimacy as a leader in the organization.

The Importance of Decisive Decision-Making

We finish this discussion on the Stabilization phase by highlighting the importance of taking decisive action. CIOs emphasize that decisions should be made quickly in this phase in order to overcome organizational inertia. In the Entry phase, we recommend avoiding feeling the pressure to make quick decisions that is likely to result in significant disruption. As we described, this doesn't mean to delay urgent matters, but rather to moderate the desire to make an immediate impression. When hard decisions are required, however, decisive action must be taken. No amount of "learning" in the Entry phase will provide all of the information necessary to make hard decisions comfortable.

The CIO of the Air Ambulance Service who invested her time explaining her actions and priorities to her team had this to share:

I think the one mistake that I made … is wait as long as I did to make obvious staff changes that needed to be made. So, I knew pretty quickly some of the staffing changes that needed to be made, but because I was trying to establish that relationship and build a rapport, I waited probably 3 months longer than I should have. I waited until about the sixth month mark to start to make some key staff changes and I won't do that again because it was detrimental to the overall team.

The comment by a CIO from the gaming industry demonstrates the overlapping nature of the Stabilization and Entry phase. Even as a new CIO is learning about the organization, they must also be acting on identifying where urgent change might be needed:

> I think it's important to put your stamp on the organization reasonably early but not rushing through it. So, identify where the problems are, whether it is structure, process, whatever it might be, and very quickly put plans in place to address those.

Our study participants shared that executives need to be able to make decisions with insufficient information and to acknowledge that some of those decisions will turn out to be bad ones (or at least not as good as anticipated!). In that case, the important thing is to avoid dwelling on it and move on:

> [A]s CIOs we make decisions. Whether those decisions are good or bad decisions can take a little while to play out. When you invest in a particular technology, it can take a year before you find out if it was a good or bad decision. CIO—Electronics Distribution Company

> I keep telling my team it's easier to make a change from movement as opposed to getting started. So, we can just get started. Not making a decision is worse than making one you have to change. If you make the wrong decision, then you made the wrong decision and you adjust and ask for forgiveness later. CIO—Petroleum Refining Company

> I would say, trust your gut. You got into a leadership position for a reason and I think I had a tendency to want a lot more information, a lot more validation that the decision was the right one, before I executed on it. You have to be able to execute quickly with limited information and you just learn to trust your gut. I think the right answer too late is worse than the wrong answer early. CIO—Electric Power Utility

> It's better to make a decision and adjust later if necessary than not making a decision at all. CIO—Apparel Manufacturer

In the Entry phase, CIOs develop a course of action with the recommendation to delay big decisions during their first 90–100 days. After this plan has been developed, according to experienced CIOs, taking decisive action is a factor in a successful Stabilization phase. They recognize that decisions often have to be made with insufficient information with the knowledge that corrective actions can be taken if the outcome is not satisfactory. It is more important at this point not to delay taking action. Taking decisions, making adjustments when desired effects are not realized and moving on are common leadership qualities of CIOs. The most complete description of this was shared by this experienced CIO of a pharmaceutical manufacturer:

> I've made a gazillion mistakes in this job. A ton of them! I would like to think that I have made more right decisions than wrong decisions along the way, but it's not—it's not 9 out of 10 decisions are right, it's probably more like 7 out of 10 on some days. I believe if you don't make decisions, don't move things forward then— or attempt to move them forward—then you're dead in the water. And that's probably what I see when I put new people in higher level roles, that there is a sense of paranoia of being wrong, especially if you get up into the organization, to the director and VP role. In people's minds, and I think I went through the same thing, thinking, oh I'm at this level so I've got to always be right and you don't. You just got to be—you've got to adjust when you're wrong. And you've not got to spend a whole lot of time fleeting over the fact you were wrong. And that's across the board—that's whether it's a technology decision, it's a funding decision, it's a people decision. Nobody gets it right all the time. I think it's the ones that can acknowledge that quickly and change and move on are the ones that will be successful.

There are several key outcomes of the Stabilization phase. One is that the CIO gains credibility through effective delivery of IT services and projects. Stabilizing the organization's operational backbone lays the critical foundation required for digital transformation. Digital technologies cannot be exploited for customer value if the operational (e.g. ERP) systems and service delivery excellence is not in place. The other key outcomes are that the CIO builds their own IT leadership team and implements basic IT governance processes. Implementing fundamental IT governance processes sets boundaries with top executive peers with regard to IT investment decisions and prioritization. By building their own leadership team, the CIO creates a group of leaders who buy into their vision and are capable of delivering strategic initiatives to the business. One Silicon Valley CIO summed up his current assignment this way:

> We're getting a lot of early wins in the first 9 months. By month 3 the attrition in IT went to zero and the team is re-energized by this new perspective of IT, that we're bringing in exciting technology and they are feeling good about what we're doing in IT.

The Renewal Phase

The Renewal phase is characterized by the CIOs building on their credibility to implement changes, particularly in respect of delivery and meeting any promises that position them to be seen as a legitimate business leader. In this phase, they focus on contributing more to the strategic direction of the organization. Renewal normally starts somewhere between months 12 and 18 and builds on the work begun in the Stabilization phase, enhancing the IT leadership team and reshaping the organization's IT governance processes. This is the essence of CIO leadership that exemplifies the CIO as a business executive with special responsibility for information and technology.

Setting Strategic Direction

One objective for any CIO is to establish the capability to lead the organization to explore new IT-driven business opportunities that will lead to organizational innovations, and business growth.[4] This requires getting closer to the business by understanding stakeholder objectives and priorities and build on 'supply-side' credibility to create the legitimacy to influence the strategic discourse in the C-suite. CIOs describe this in two ways. One is focused on establishing a strategy for information and technology that clearly highlights the contribution of both.

> Lots of people say that they have an IT strategy, but it's stuck up in someone's head. [A CIO needs to] lead, communicate that, talk to your peers about it and that's really valuable. It makes IT more accessible to business leaders. CIO—Electronics Distributor

> One of my objectives was to put a clear IT strategy together for the Group. I hired a consultant who helped me frame it and document it and communicate it in the right way to the executive team. I spent a lot of time communicating that down to my organization as well. CIO—Video Processor Manufacturer

The other is how non-IT business leaders viewed the IT function's contribution.

> My first year was getting an IT strategy documented and really getting a road map back in front from a technology perspective. Also getting a good story so we could reach out to our sales and delivery guys and say: 'we can help here.' They were used to IT as a service provider and order taker. Expectations were low. Now as we've transformed it you know, more and more people come to ask, 'hey can you help us here, why can't we move faster there.' CIO—Professional Services Firm

> The Customer Development function had the wrong strategy just as I was taking the job, so I've been very involved in crafting the new strategy. That buys you a lot of credibility when the Chief Customer Development Officer points to you and says he has figured out how technology is part of his strategy moving forward. CIO—Global Consumer Products Manufacturer

The businesspeople on the retail side of the business never had anyone who told them or indicated that technology can drive significant improvements or efficiencies or anything like that. IT has never really been a business partner but we have turned that around. CIO—Gaming Industry

Setting a more strategic direction for IT and ITs contribution to the business objectives is a key activity in the Renewal phase. After building the team in the Stabilization phase, CIOs now make growing the capability of the team a priority. By-in-large, this is accomplished by increasing the business savvy of the team as well as formal professional development programs.

I always think of my senior team. I try to give them the kind of exposure so they could learn and nothing would please me more than every one of my direct reports would go on to become CIO somewhere else. CIO—Electronics Distributor

Six months after I started, we started a rotation where on any given day, there are a number of IT team members sitting in the middle of one of our sales or call centers doing calls with our sales agents. So, it garnered credibility for the IT teams and also forced a different type of interaction. It's interesting to see the dynamics have shifted. CIO—Video Processor Manufacturer

I sent our entire IT leadership team through Covey[5] training; we did effective presentation and effective negotiations training. We're bringing in executive coaches to work with a lot of the [IT] leadership [team]. I continue to tell them we need people capable of working with the business to help them and be consultants to them. CIO—Professional Services Firm

We got a lot of IT people out into the business. So, they learned what those people were doing and actually spent a week at a time with the territory salespeople. CIO—Hand Tool Manufacturer

Talent is one of the most important things, at least to a large-scale IT shop, and you're never done. It's kind of like take your favorite sports metaphor, the team has just won the Super Bowl, you know what, they're going through their roster saying who is not on the team next year and what are our weaknesses and who do we need new. CIO—Global Consulting Firm

CIOs try to raise the IT savvy of their business partners by demonstrating how IT can help them achieve their goals as well as one-on-one coaching. The objective is to develop the frame of reference (FoR) of the senior leadership team to better recognize the role that information technology plays in the strategy of the organization. It changes assumptions that IT is very tactical in nature to how IT can contribute competitive advantage. This has the virtuous result of also enhancing the IT governance processes and improving the relationship of the CIO to the rest of the senior leadership team because it creates a positive view of the CIO and the IT organization as a whole.

> I think there is a lot one can do to build deeper IT savvy and it requires investing in relationships with each of the executives you know. So, a combination of one-on-one meetings and gravitating to the people who understood the power [of information technology]. CIO—Hand Tool Manufacturer

CIOs can also use "brown bag" lunches as well as one-on-one coaching.

> It is one of my ambitions to educate and get people excited about technology … as an enabler and something that adds real business value. There is a lot of one-on-one coaching as well as some group stand-up activities. I think in the U.S. you call them 'brown bags,' lunches and stuff like that where people can turn up and listen. We have done sessions on mobile and how mobile is transforming our business and other businesses, that kind of stuff. We tried a few different things. CIO—Gaming Organization

In general, CIOs are less ambitious about increasing the IT savvy of the C-suite via formal educational processes. While these formal sessions are viewed as positive, they are not seen as having the biggest impact. The most impactful way to change their peers' FoR is to demonstrate that IT projects can contribute business value. They focus their time initially on their peers who are already open to incorporating information technology to accomplish their business objectives. In this way they attempt to raise awareness among the other top management team of how information technology might help them as well by showcasing real examples.

Enhancing IT Governance

Another area of continuing enhancement comes in IT governance processes. One CIO describes moving the process to focus more on business value rather than risk in making IT investment decisions. The basic IT governance processes established in the Stabilization phase provide the foundation on which to further enhance those processes in the Renewal phase.

> We've put the steps in place now that over the next few weeks we'll start with—as we start our portfolio reviews, we're prioritizing more to value and we've gone through and done some of the quantification of value. That drastically changes the way we look at the portfolio or what's most important versus not, and that

I think is going to drive to probably initially a lot of friction but a much healthier discussion with our business partners. Because what we're trying to get to is using value, whether top line or bottom-line, how do we go about quantifying that by getting better and better at quantifying value to help us stop doing things that aren't driving value which we've traditionally struggled with—actually all IT shops struggle with that. CIO—Apparel Retailer

CIOs introduce change in terms of IT governance processes and the CxOs' perception of the value of IT while working within the cultural constraints of the organization. CIOs recognize that there is a finite capacity for change within an organization and that they need to pace the speed of change according to that cultural capacity.

The Emerging Business Leader

The most significant transition for the CIO in the Renewal phase is to gain legitimacy as a business leader. This is demonstrating business leadership for the new CIO and is how they operate as a fully functional member of the executive leadership team.

The CEO said to me 'I love all the directions you gave us on IT, your guidance and collaboration. But you have more to offer so don't just limit yourself to having a view on IT related topics. We need to hear more from you'. CIO—Electronics Distributor

I think the best advice I got was from this VP who said 'forget that you're an IT guy, from this day forward you are a business guy.' CIO—Hand Tool Manufacturer

CIOs experience this in their interactions with the CEO and peer executives in the top team. The result of building relationships, the topic of Chap. 8, is a way to demonstrate this leadership. These CIO leaders sometimes represent the senior leadership team to others in the organization with regard to the organization's strategic plans.

My boss in the senior leadership team uses me to go out to our remote sites and articulate our strategic vision as a company. Now, that's kind of weird for the IT guy to be the one doing that. CIO—Semi-conductor Manufacturer

I spend about two hours a week with our CEO talking about operating models and what the things are that we're doing and how those implications of those decisions impact the business and the business operating model which has been extraordinarily helpful for me and I think for him as well because it's changed the way he talks about some components of our business. CIO—Apparel Retailer

The CIO of a semi-conductor manufacturer mentioned that he was still learning this new role.

> I still have a lot to learn about becoming a more influential member of the executive staff. I'm acknowledging and responding to issues and participating in the conversation. I wouldn't say that I'm driving the conversation.

A significant outcome in the taking charge process for CIOs is to be integral to the business strategy of the organization and to be viewed as a business leader. The Renewal phase is characterized by the CIO building on their credibility to implement changes that position them to become a legitimate business leader. These changes are often in the form of digital transformation in the form of digitized products, processes, services or even new business models. The CIO enhances the capability of the IT leadership team and improves IT governance processes. They exert influence in setting IT strategy and start the evolution from IT leader to business leader.

Taking the Reins

The period required to take charge is much more than the first 90 days; it is a process of three phases that occur over the course of 24–36 months. Each phase has a unique duration, set of activities and outcomes. There are a number of focal areas that thread throughout all three phases, with activities in these areas become more sophisticated as time goes on. A plan for the first 90–100 days is important, but not nearly sufficient. A new CIO needs to be as intentional and systematic in planning for the first and second years of their tenure as they are for the first 90 days. The plan needs to consider the key activities outlined here and the required outcomes of each phase. Of course, much of what happens will be dictated by the transition type.

Through the phases of taking charge, the CIO progresses from understanding to credibility as the IT leader and eventually being recognized as a business leader with special responsibility for IT. The evolution from IT leader to be recognized as a business leader is dependent on the CIO's performance in the Stabilization and Renewal phases. It is also highly influenced by the CIO's peers and the relationship with them. We explore the CxO perspective and CIO/CxO relationships in the following two chapters.

Notes

1. Research recommends that if you are a manager making a transition to a leadership role, quick wins should not be about your personal scoreboard or pet project but about your management of a group of individuals. A focus on collective quick wins ensures that your work as a leader is a success. See M.E. Van Buren and T. Safferstone, 'The quick win paradox', *Harvard Business Review*, January, 2009, pp. 55–61.

2. There is significant research showing a positive relationship between the presence of IT governance processes and mechanisms and organizational performance. See, for example, P. Weill and J. Ross, *IT Governance: How Top Managers Manage IT Decision Rights for Superior Results*, Boston: Harvard Business School Press, 2004 and S. Wu, D. Straub and T.P. Liang, 'How information technology governance mechanisms and strategic alignment influence organizational performance: Insights from a matched survey of business and IT managers', *MIS Quarterly*, Vol. 39, No. 2, 2015, pp. 497–518.

3. There are also academic studies supporting this position. See D.A. Marchand, W.J. Kettinger and J.D. Rollins, 'Information orientation: People, technology and the bottom line', *Sloan Management Review*, Vol. 41, 2000, pp. 69–80 and J. Peppard, 'Unlocking the performance of the chief information officer (CIO)', *California Management Review*, Vol. 52, No. 4, 2010, pp. 73–99.

4. D. Chen, D.S. Preston, and W. Xia, 'Antecedents and effects of CIO supply-side and demand-side leadership: A staged maturity model', *Journal of Management Information Systems*, Vol. 27, 2010, pp. 231–271.

5. S.R. Covey, *The 7 Habits of Highly Effective People: Powerful Lessons in Personal Change*, Simon and Schuster, 2004.

7

The Other Side of the Coin

While the experience of CIOs themselves is incredibly insightful, it is not the complete story. As we have seen, other senior executives in the organization—the other side of the coin—influence the taking charge process and, consequently, whether the CIO is successful or not. This led us to speak with non-IT executives to discern their attitudes toward CIOs and their experiences working with and observing CIOs and how their views and the perspectives they hold can help and hinder CIOs as they take charge.

We saw in Chap. 3 that taking charge can be described as a process of organizational socialization. This can be explained simply as "learning the ropes" of the new role and about the organization and its key stakeholders. Understanding "how we do things around here" and "fitting in" are also important in adjusting to a new situation. We noted that the research on socialization and role theory describes the influence of "role-senders" in the process of taking charge, with members of a role-set (a peer group) influencing other members of the group.[1] "Role-senders" are typically those who have a vested interest in the newcomer's transition.[2] These role-senders also communicate information and send signals regarding appropriate behavior and cultural norms within the organization. In the case of the CIO, members of their role-set are colleagues in the C-suite. The primary role-sender for the CIO will probably be the CEO, contingent on the reporting structure in the organization. Of course, reporting into a CFO may present a different set of circumstances for the CIO to deal with.

The first phase of the taking charge process is principally concerned with learning. This includes deciphering the viewpoints and positions that are held by colleagues regarding information and technology. While glimpses of these

© The Author(s) 2020
T. Gerth, J. Peppard, *Taking the Reins as CIO*,
https://doi.org/10.1007/978-3-030-31953-3_7

might have been observed prior to joining the organization it is only when in situ that a more comprehensive frame of reference (FoR) can be gleaned for different individuals. This FoR captures an executive's assumptions about the role of information and technology and what it takes to be successful in today's digital world, their expectation for the CIO through to their appetite to engage with the CIO and technology-related issues. The challenge for a CIO is that their peers may not have similar FoRs. This might mean that their vision for the future differs or beliefs about what it will take for success diverge. It might also signal that some may be less receptive to any overtures that the CIO may make. All these can present a significant barrier to overcome when trying to push initiatives that demand change and engagement and support that may not align with an executive's FoR. As the CIO builds relationships and enhances their credibility with colleagues, they can then begin on embarking on ways to influence them and effectively amend their FoR.

CxO Perceptions of the CIO Role

We have noted on numerous occasions the ambiguous nature of the CIO role and this was only confirmed by the executives we spoke to. They expressed a variety of different views of the role and described varying expectations for a CIO. This only serves to make the CIO's job incredibly difficult as they can be working with colleagues who can each have a different viewpoint regarding both the role and the expectations they have for their new colleague.

Rather than engage in a definitional debate, what we were interested in was understanding whether the different viewpoints impacted the degree of strategic influence a CIO would have. (I think that we already knew the answer to this question before analyzing our data!) The different characterizations of the role enabled us to develop three broad categories based on the degree of strategic influence assigned by colleagues to a CIO. These categories are Service Provider, Solution Provider and Strategic Contributor (see Fig. 7.1).

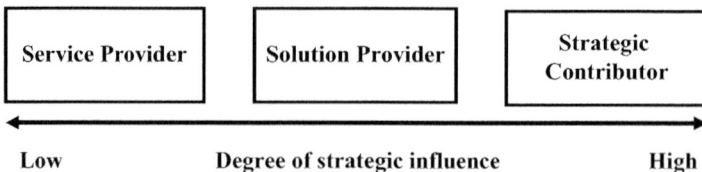

Fig. 7.1 CIO roles described by non-IT executives. (Source: Based on A.B. Gerth and J. Peppard, 'The dynamics of CIO derailment: How CIOs come undone and how to avoid it', *Business Horizons*, Vol. 59, No. 1, 2016, pp. 61–70)

These perspectives are not defined by the organizational structure or the CIO's reporting level, but rather the personal perspective of the executive. Each executive interviewed had one of these categories in mind for particular CIOs that they had worked with. The variety of viewpoints we encountered can be gleaned from some interview quotes:

> They [CIOs] have to have the recognition that they are a servant to the organization, and they're not in charge of everything. They are a servant to the organization to serve the customers. You've got to be an internal consultant, asking all the right questions. They have to have that attitude of servant's heart within the company so that when they talk to that other guy who's running that division or that geographical area, or that department, or whatever it is, that they have to serve an interface with … That person feels like 'this guy's my resource. This guy's not telling me how it is'. Chairman—Insurance and Brokerage Firm

> I think the successful ones are integrated and understand business and their real objectives that they are not really about technology, they are about—and I keep using the term—ensuring that technology they're delivering enables the company to do something with it whether it be close the books, serve the customer. I think that high quality Chief Information Officers are those who are integrated as part of senior management and understand the responsibilities that they have to bring technology to the business and serve a purpose whether it be financial processes, customer service, operations, inventory management, all of those things that link together. EVP & CFO—Natural Gas Distribution Organization

> It's a pretty thankless task. When things don't go well, everybody notices. When things are going well, people see that's how it should be anyway. SVP and COO—Retail Analytics Firm

> As we develop our strategy and is there a systems component to that that we're going to need to allow us to sell more products, to be more productive in our factories … Then I think they're very involved. But in starting to lay out what the strategy is or any modifications to the strategy, they're probably the last person you look to for input. CEO—Diversified Manufacturer

> [H]e [new CIO] really did a great job of reaching out to all the leaders to really try to understand, 'How are you using IT? I'm here to help us further and advance tools that can help us from a technology standpoint to better do our jobs, and ultimately deliver what we need to in terms of expectations'. Global Marketing V.P.—Food Products Retailer

The *Service Provider* is defined by a low degree of strategic influence and an expectation among executives that emphasizes providing services to their part of the business. These executives view the CIO role as primarily concerned with determining and delivering services and the IT unit as a support function. While they may appreciate the complexity of IT and the challenge that presents for the CIO, they do not view the role as equal to other operating executives. Their wish is not to be inconvenienced by IT. They generally do not expect strategic input from the CIO, nor do they necessarily want it. The extent of their expectations is for the CIO keep the applications and infrastructure running smoothly and to "fix" their IT problems.

The CIO as *Solution Provider* type is characterized by them having a higher degree of strategic influence. Executives describe the Service Provider in terms of designing and delivering "solutions" to business issues. These executives expect that they would present business problems to the CIO and that he/she will find IT solutions to address these problems. They also expect the CIO to actively understand their problems and behave like a consultant or business partner in designing solutions for them. In contrast to the Service Provider, the executives who view the CIO as a Solutions Provider have a greater degree of respect for the role and an expectation that the CIO will engage with business problems and issues in addition to technical ones.

The *Strategic Contributor* is viewed by other executives as a peer in the leadership team. In addition to providing IT solutions and services, they expect the CIO to engage with them in strategic conversations and help in driving IT-enabled change. They expect the CIO to act as a strategic advisor to operating executives, proactively bringing ideas enabled by technology that have the potential to influence both operational and strategic performance. This strategic contribution is becoming more valuable as organizations undergo digital transformations and look to harness the capabilities of leading technologies.

These three categories describe a "maturity model" of sorts for how CIOs are viewed in organizations. Our research and that of others clearly indicate that CIOs will struggle to influence strategic initiatives until they have demonstrated effective leadership of the IT function.[3] In other words, CIOs need to demonstrate they are managing the IT assets and services of the organization in an efficient and effective way before their peers will recognize them as legitimate business leaders who can participate in strategic discussions; this is essentially the objective of the Stabilization and Renewal phases of the taking charge process. These categories also follow a cumulative trajectory. A CIO viewed as a Solution Provider is also expected to be an effective Service Provider. Similarly, a CIO who is a Strategic Contributor will also be an accomplished Solution and Service Provider.

Where it starts to get a bit tricky for the CIO is that it is possible to be confronted with a C-suite that inhabit all three categories. Our CIOs agreed that they always need to provide excellent service and solutions for the organization. Moving into the strategic contributor role requires a systematic process of delivering value for the right stakeholders. In the next chapter, we will explore a framework for identifying, prioritizing and influencing peer relationships in light of these different frames of reference.

What Makes for a Successful Transition?

We also asked CxOs to describe the difference between a successful and unsuccessful CIO transition into the organization. While different opinions were expressed—as might be expected—three stood out. The first is achieving results, basically performing one's expected job functions and meeting expectations. The second factor is achieving these results in a way that is culturally acceptable. The final factor is the quality of the relationships the CIO develops with other executives. In the remainder of this section, we will look in a little more detail at the first two factors, achieving results and cultural fit. Given the importance of CIO peer relationships, we devote the entire next chapter to this topic.

Getting Results

Achieving results is acknowledged as "obviously" necessary for success. This is consistent with the description of the Stabilization phase of taking charge we described earlier. One key outcome of that phase is building credibility as a leader. This is the result of understanding the business and the CIO's role in the organization to properly execute those projects successfully. This assumes there is a shared understanding of what "success" looks like and this is often not the case!

We dug a bit deeper and asked executives how they assess the success of an IT investment. The word "investment" was purposely used rather than "project", as it implies a commercially or mission-oriented expression of value that exceeds the sum invested. The executives in our research varied widely in their perspectives on what constituted a successful investment. They frequently did not have an immediate answer to the question and several commented that the question "was a hard one". Generally, IT investment success was described in two different ways: project success: on budget, on time, meet requirements and that the system is being used; business success: the organization realized the planned benefits and outcomes.

Project success was typically described as follows:

> Success is ultimately—the system is adopted and used by the organization. The second is, was it done on time and was it done within in budget. V.P. Sales—Plastic Products Manufacturing

> Are the IT applications really serving the purpose they were designed for? EVP and CFO—Natural Gas Distribution Company

By far the most common description of "success" was focused on achieving business outcomes; this is encouraging. These benefits were described in a number of different ways, illustrating the broad range of benefits that can be realized from an IT investment. Efficiency, cost reduction, labor savings, inventory reduction, customer satisfaction, inventory accuracy, increasing revenue and customer value are just some of those mentioned. In addition, executives described initiating investments in information technology for agility, cybersecurity, regulatory, compliance and other strategic reasons without having specific financial metrics of success.

When asked if their organization did a good job of realizing those planned benefits the overwhelmingly response was negative. Most executives reported that their current organization and others with which they were familiar did not do well at realizing the benefits from IT investments.

> I would say less than 20% of the time [executives determine whether an IT project delivered the planned benefits]. I think if they've got the new thing up and running, and it doesn't cause major disruption to the objectives, most business executive's view that as adequate performance, which is kind of a shame. Regional V.P.—Telecommunications Company

> Nobody does that [benefits realization] well. Nobody does a post implementation analysis either. V.P. Private Brands—Retailer

> I would say almost universally I'm not really aware of many organizations at all that, once the business case is done, later on actually do go back and check the business case and see if what they thought they would get out of it is what they actually got. I'm aware of very few of those. But everybody is aware of when something works and doesn't work. At least to my knowledge, companies are extremely bad in actually doing that [checking that the expected business outcomes have actually been delivered]. SVP and COO—Professional Services Firm

There were some exceptions:

We track them [project benefits], we measure them and … we follow them through their life generally. V.P. Strategy—Logistics and Distribution

We would measure cost savings. CEO—Diversified Industrial Manufacturing

I've seen our company do a pretty good job of validating outcomes after the fact if the intended outcomes were actually achieved. President—Banking and Finance Institution

The question of where responsibilities lie for achieving benefits generated polarized views. There were those that were strongly of the view that responsibility resided with IT. There were interesting comments from executives that they felt "IT" was responsible for this lack of follow-up rather than the business executive themselves.

Rarely did I see, you know, as you start a new year, a new planning cycle, never did the IT group come in and give you post-analysis. V.P. Private Brands—Retailer

I think IT can do better. I think the people that are directly involved in the project particularly on the IT side have a pretty big vested interest in painting a picture that might be rosier than it is. So, I think there is room for improvement there. V.P. Sales—Security Systems Products Manufacturer

One company that uses information technology strategically and where the executive described the executive team IT savvy as "sophisticated" commented:

They [benefits realization] get handed off, once they go from IT to the business owner or the functional group that's responsible. Then through a mechanism of accountability they are tracked, monitored and reviewed on a periodic basis. V.P. Strategy—Logistics and Distribution Company

There was an acknowledgment that sometimes determining the successful achievement of business benefits was difficult, if not impossible, to do quantitatively.

Success is ultimately if it is adopted and used by the organization and that it has improved working before the project. That's the ultimate one. The second is, was it done on time and was it done within in budget. I think what we do is, if the pain is reduced and people sense that, that's almost good enough in a lot of cases. V.P. Sales—Plastic Products Manufacturer

I guess the decision-making process, do you have 80% of it pretty hard cost as best you can, and the other 20% as sort of instinct and seat of the pants, and just feeling that that's the right way to go. Chairman—Insurance and Brokerage Firm

There's not a full post-implementation audit. There is an intuitive, a general feel, you know, have the troops quieted down? Managing Director—Banking and Finance Institution

You try to look at the project as it stands and then have some metrics that address that individual project as opposed to … what's my return. I think at times there are metrics, and I think there are times when you actually can do some quantification, but it's never precise. Managing Director—Banking and Finance Institution

We're saying IT applications investments in almost all case should pay for itself and there's a whole lot of reasons why they don't, but they're business reasons generally … What they don't understand is exactly what the impact will be on the business. If the goal is to reduce the inventory by increasing inventory turns exactly what does that mean and how do [executives] come up with a plan that'll establish the base case that allows them to establish the methods that they're going to use to track the program and ultimately how are they going to know whether they succeeded or failed. I've talked about The Christopher Columbus School of Management. Mr. Columbus went on a great trip, didn't know where he was going, got there, didn't know where he was, he came back, and didn't know where he'd been. Director Operations—Chemical Manufacturer

By far the most dominant way executives assessed the success of an IT investment was based on adherence to budget, schedule achievement, satisfied users and delivery of functionality. Perhaps surprisingly, few viewed the realization of benefits and business outcomes as a measure of success and far fewer of those evaluated what was achieved after the new IT solution went live. This suggests that perhaps many executives still under-value the contribution that IT makes to the business because their focus is primarily on project metrics rather than business results, reflecting their FoR.

The IT organization was mentioned most often as being responsible for ensuring investment success even when success was described as delivering planned business outcomes and benefits. This is consistent with observations made that business executives often do not understand their role in achieving value from IT spending.[4] Studies have highlighted that, in the absence of more quantitative measures, executives' *perceptions* of success are equally or more important.[5]

The findings are also consistent with an earlier study of executive perceptions of the business value of IT.[6] This research found that the use of pre-investment and post-investment evaluation was correlated with the corporate goals for IT (operations focused, unfocused, market focus or dual focus). Organizations with a higher strategic positioning (market and dual focus) were more likely to use post-investment evaluations in establishing business value achieved.

This is significant because delivering results was one of the factors that executives overwhelmingly mentioned contributed to the successful transition for a newly appointed CIO. Delivering results is about delivering business value through IT services and projects. If the standard measure of success depends on each individual executive's perspective, then the CIO may have difficulty fulfilling what might be a wide range of expectations. Previous research found evidence that conflict regarding the value of IT can be specific to subunits in the organization and that those units are influenced by the most powerful person in the group.[7] To compound the matter, the IT organization is frequently seen as the responsible party for delivering success, regardless of its definition.

We discussed previously that delivering successful IT initiatives in the Stabilization and Renewal phases resulted in, respectively, credibility and legitimacy for the newly appointed CIO. Therefore, it is critical for the CIO to set and manage expectations of success before the IT investment is delivered. If the senior leadership of the organization views success as meeting budget, schedule and expected functionality then the CIO must align to those metrics or negotiate something different. Negotiating IT performance measures will create a shared understanding among all executives on how the success of an IT investment will be evaluated. It will not benefit the CIO to focus solely on realizing business benefits (sometimes at the expense of project budget or schedule), if the rest of the organization views budget and schedule as priorities. Setting clear objectives that all agree upon for the CIO to achieve is critical to be viewed as delivering results; but sometimes to do this, an executive's FoR may need to be adjusted. Delivering these results will contribute to the newly appointed CIO's successful transition.

Cultural Fit

The second success factor highlighted by CxOs for CIOs for a successful transition was fitting into the organization's culture and doing things the "right way". Culture was described on numerous occasions as the "way things are done around here" and includes familiarity with an organization's unique vocabulary.

I've made mistakes thinking that when I transition from one company to another thinking that I can do the same thing that I did at the previous company the same way, getting the same results, assuming they were successful, and found out that wasn't the case because the culture was really different. Then you've got to come up with a different method of implementation or process of implementation because what works at one place does not necessarily work at another. V.P. Operations—Wire and Cable Manufacturing Company

So, I think understanding the vocabulary, the hot buttons, just quickly being able to understand what those are, to learn the new culture that way. CEO— Diversified Industrial Manufacturing Company

From an IT perspective or any function, you know you have a job to do, so you want to come in, hit the ground running, start moving forward and make things happen, right? Because everyone's pretty much results driven across many fronts. And it takes I think a lot of discipline to be able to come in and be able to say, 'Okay, I really need to build a relationship.' And a key component of that is to be able to listen, to understand the culture of the business, the players, so that you can then effectively think about, 'How can I transition successfully?' So, I think for those who probably don't do as well are those who do the exact opposite of that. Director-Global Marketing—Food Products Manufacturer

Are they prepared to be the team player and you know, play nice in the sandbox, be collegial, you know, don't have a star system etc. He'll put in the hours regardless of what's required type of mentality, which we have here. You need to understand the culture and what's valued in that culture and you need to model that behavior. So, you better have done your homework before you join because that's where you need to be—you need to model the successful executives and the culture and take that up or else, you know, you're gonna be an odd duck. Managing Director—Banking and Finance Institution

Successful CIO transitions are accomplished by "doing the right things the right way" as one executive described it. This consists of delivering results and fitting into the culture of the organization. This is especially true with regard to digital initiatives. Often, digital projects require significant organizational change. There are clearly organizational nuances that are important for the newly appointed CIO to recognize. These are how success is evaluated, how to fit into the organization's culture and building effective peer relationships (the subject of the next chapter). Gaining this knowledge is important to the CIO entering a new organization.

Uncovering Frames of Reference

Building a shared vision across the leadership team of the potential role of information and technology can sometimes take time and is not without its frustrations. This is particularly so if the CIO is seeking to take the organization in a direction which demands significant organizational change and their belief for what it will take for success does not align with that of their new colleagues. Of course, each executive team member will have his/her own individual perspective and these may not be fully aligned across the C-suite. As might be expected, this situation can lead to a complicated scenario for the incoming CIO.

In order to build consensus, the newly appointed CIO must discern their peer's baseline understanding of how information and technology either enables or could enable the organization to achieve its strategic and operational objectives. For example, if the CIO has ambitions to drive a digital agenda that will challenge existing structures, processes, ways of working, accountabilities and funding, how amenable will colleagues be to support the change that will inevitably be required. They must also discern their appetite for any changes that many need to be made, particularly those that will impact their area of responsibility.

No CxO today is not going to acknowledge the tremendous impact that technology has for competitions or not buy into the need for organizations to "do things differently". Executives recognize the role of data and potential it has. However, CIOs report that their real challenge often begins when it comes to putting in place what need to happen for any vision to be realized.

While the CxOs we spoke to generally had a positive perspective of their own IT savvy, many acknowledged that they felt that they had still much to learn. Those that did consider themselves well versed, when probed, the extent of their IT savvy meant a recognition of both the impact and potential of technology and how it was shaping industries. We found that really understanding what it takes to be successful with information and technology was generally lacking.

We did encounter executives who acknowledge the disruptive potential of technology, see the CIO role as encompassing strategy and innovation but still treated the CIO as a Service Provider. Failing to see the paradox of their viewpoint, they wanted their CIO to be a miracle worker and achieve major impact without having to trouble them!

In one survey of global CIOs that we conducted, we asked CIOs about their perception of the levels of digital literacy—using this concept as a surrogate of their FoR—they encountered in working with C-level colleagues. A significant number reported that their colleagues were ill-equipped to embrace digitization and engage in the necessary conversations.

In follow-up interviews, some CIOs lamented that for many of their colleagues, their understanding of digital was based on their experience with consumer IT; yet, consumer IT does not equate to enterprise IT. Expecting everything to be like consumer IT shows a lack of understanding of the challenges and issues that IT poses within a corporate environment.[8] More worrying, their experience with consumer IT is also giving executives a strong argument for opting out of any involvement in decisions regarding IT. In the consumer world, all digital services are vanilla versions; the exact same service is available to all users. In the corporate world, expecting users to "just live" with a new way of working is often the downfall of many IT projects. While a vanilla version of a software application can be acceptable, and many corporations use standard versions of ERP software from major vendors, any choice should be a business decision made by business managers for operational and strategic reasons. Crucially, these are not technical decisions made by a CIO, although they may be part of the decision-making process.

There is some irony in this observation regarding executives' familiarity with technology. A previous research study reported that CIOs *"hinted that executive's personal use of computers may work to the CIO's disadvantage, as executives who are strong computer users sometimes become overconfident about their understanding of IT"*.[9] This quote is from several decades ago! Yet it expresses a contemporary situation described by the executives in our research. Only the technology has changed!

In most situations, CIOs will have to influence other top managers to support and engage with strategic IT investments. It is crucial that the executives are involved with IT initiatives to increase the probability of realizing the planned business value from such investments.[10] However, a leadership challenge for the CIO is securing the engagement and active participation of business colleagues in matters and issues relating to information and technology. Barriers to gaining this commitment from other executives have been reported to result from bringing IT projects not related to business strategy, using technical rather than business language, and not creating a compelling case for change.[11] Communicating a compelling, business focused case for change is consistent with a study of CIOs gaining commitment from the business for new, innovative IT initiatives.[12]

The CIO should be seeking answers to the following questions to help them build a FoR profile for each member of the leadership team.

- View of CIO role and degree of strategic influence
- Expectations
- Understanding of what it takes to be successful with technology
- Willingness to engage

In addition, the CIO has to figure out the politics of the organization. Who really are the key influencers? Who has the ear of the CEO?

What CxOs Think Is Important for Success

Executives do believe they have a role to play on-boarding a CIO. The perspectives on how they enacted that role varied between those who saw their role as a passive one and those who felt an active approach was valuable. This dynamic is developed into a stakeholder framework in the next chapter.

This chapter introduced our observations from interviewing executive level leaders about information technology and CIOs. We identified a common gap between how the CIO views the IT savvy of the executive team and how individual executive team members self-identifies in terms of IT savvy. Developing a shared understanding of IT's role and a positive FoR for non-IT executives is also critical to CIO success in taking charge. Project success is an important factor influencing the CIO's success and there are a variety of definitions of success, although most focus on budget, schedule and functionality. A CIO must proactively manage the expectations of the executive team and define project success in a realistic manner. This is critical, because the consequence of delivering on project commitments is that the CIO is perceived as a credible leader.

Fitting into the culture was described as "doing the right things the right way". Business executives often described the importance of good working relationships between themselves and the CIO. In fact, the most often cited reason for a CIO's failure was lack of soft skills and ignoring peer relationships. In the next chapter, we tackle this issue with some additional insights from executives as well as guidance for the CIO on developing relationships and exerting influence.

Notes

1. R.K. Merton, 'The role-set: Problems in sociological theory', *The British Journal of Sociology*, Vol. 8, 1957, pp. 106–120.
2. See G. Graen, 'Role-making processes within complex organizations', in: M.D. Dunnette, ed., *Handbook of Industrial and Organizational Psychology*,

Rand-McNally, Chicago, 1976 and also D. Katz and R.L. Kahn, *The Social Psychology of Organizations*, New York, Wiley, 1978.

3. See D. Smaltz, V. Sambamurthy and R. Agarwal, 'The antecedents of CIO role effectiveness in organizations: An empirical study in the healthcare sector', *IEEE Transactions on Engineering Management*, Vol. 53, No. 2, 2006, pp. 207–222; D. Preston, D. Chen and D. Leidner, 'Examining the antecedents and consequences of CIO strategic decision-making authority: An empirical study', *Decision Sciences*, 39, 2008a, pp. 605–642 and D. Chen, D. Preston and W. Xia, 'Antecedents and effects of CIO supply-side and demand-side leadership: A staged maturity model', *Journal of Management Information Systems*, Vol. 27, 2010, pp. 231–271.

4. H.G. Enns, S.L. Huff and B.R. Golden, 'How CIOs obtain peer commitment to strategic is proposals: Barriers and facilitators', *Journal of Strategic Information Systems*, Vol. 10, 2001, pp. 3–14.

5. S. Watts and J. Henderson, 'Innovative IT climates: CIO perspectives', *Journal of Strategic Information Systems*, 15, 2006, pp. 125–151.

6. M. Fiegener and J. Coakley, 'CIO problems and practices: "Impression management"', *Journal of Systems Management*, Vol. 46, No. 6, 1995, pp. 56–61.

7. Differentiated project success is described in, for example, A. McAfee, 'When too much it knowledge is a dangerous thing', *MIT Sloan Management Review*, Vol. 44, 2002, pp. 83–90; J. Peppard and J. Ward, 'Unlocking sustained business value from IT investments', *California Management Review*, Vol. 48, 2005, pp. 52–70 and J. Peppard, J. Ward and E. Daniel, 'Managing the realization of business benefits from IT investments', *MIS Quarterly*, Vol. 6, No. 1, 2007, pp. 1–12.

8. For more on this, see J. Peppard, 'Executives get the IT they deserve', *Harvard Business Review*, December 1, 2015. https://hbr.org/2015/12/executives-get-the-it-they-deserve

9. H.G. Enns, S.L. Huff and B.R. Golden, 'How CIOs obtain peer commitment to strategic is proposals: Barriers and facilitators', *Journal of Strategic Information Systems*, Vol. 10, 2001, pp. 3–14.

10. D.S. Preston and E. Karahanna, 'Antecedents of IS strategic alignment: A nomological network', *Information Systems Research*, Vol. 20, 2009, pp. 159–179.

11. C. Armstrong and V. Sambamurthy, 'Creating business value through information technology: The effects of Chief Information Officer and top management team characteristics', in *Proceedings of the International Conference on Information Systems*, Association for Information Systems, 1996.

12. B. Reich and I. Benbasat, 'Factors that influence the social dimension of alignment between business and information technology objectives', *MIS Quarterly*, Vol. 24, 2000, pp. 81–113.

8

Peers, Relationships and Influence

In the early chapters, we discussed the ambiguous nature of the CIO role and how the organizational context influences the taking charge process. As we demonstrated, the existence of role ambiguity is a challenge in and of itself. A further challenge is that the success of a CIO is heavily dependent on how they "fit in" with the CxO team and do whatever needs to be done to address their collective and individual issues.[1] Tackling these will require colleagues to have confidence in the CIO and for the CIO to have great deal of credibility and trust.

Early into the appointment, the CIO must discern a number of contextual factors such as the frame of reference (FoR) for information and technology success held by members of the leadership team, the effectiveness of current information and technology governance processes and the general attitude toward IT. This can identify a number of gaps between the CIO's perspective and ambition and that of their peers, creating a tension that will need to be addressed. Bridging any gaps is fundamental for the new CIO to "fit in" and requires excelling at the social processes of relationship building.

While a newly appointed CIO can, over time, shape their peers' expectations, he/she comes into an environment with pre-existing views that may be at odds with their own. In order to build the credibility and trust necessary to have influence, a CIO must determine if different perceptions exist.[2] In the previous chapter, we presented the CxO perspective of the CIO role and how they typically assess success and emphasized the importance of getting an understanding of the C-suite's FoR for information and technology. An individual's FoR will also signal their willingness to engage with the CIO and the likely nature of that engagement. Our interviews with CxOs have enabled us to build a framework suggesting broad categories of executive that a CIO might

© The Author(s) 2020
T. Gerth, J. Peppard, *Taking the Reins as CIO*,
https://doi.org/10.1007/978-3-030-31953-3_8

need to engage with. Using this, we show the types of influencing techniques that can be used and suggest how to tailor those to the different CxO types. We conclude the chapter by introducing the concept of social capital, suggesting that in the process of taking charge, CIOs are actually building and nurturing their social capital. This provides them with a valuable resource with which to get things done and thrive in the role.

Creating a Shared Understanding and Vision

In our conversations, both CIOs and CxOs emphasized the crucial importance of aligning expectations regarding the role that the CIO is being hired into. In essence, what the CIO is responsible for what lies outside of his/her remit. They also stressed the importance of there being a shared understanding and vision as to the role that information and technology will play in both the operations and strategy of the organization. CIOs noted that it is relatively easy to get colleagues enthusiastic about the digital opportunity. What is more of a challenge is getting them to buy into the changes that becoming a digital enterprise will demand.

During our interviews with CxOs, they frequently mentioned that aligning to the CEO's vision was critical to incumbents' success in the role:

> Looking at the ones that weren't so successful, in the end it always seems like it's the chemistry between the two. The CEO and the CIO were not aligned. V.P. Operations—Wire and Cable Manufacturer

> Make sure that's [his vision] part of the conversation you have with your boss, and get in line that, 'This is how I want to approach on-boarding,' and staying in line with your immediate supervisor. Director-Global Marketing—Food Products Manufacturer

> The guys and gals who come in and have been successful, are the ones that figured out very quickly the CEO's vision. SVP and COO—Professional Services Firm

Sometimes the CEOs vision for digital does not extend beyond "we need to embrace technology and become a digital company," with the CIO charged with putting the detail behind this vision (that might be the reason the hiring took place). Other times, it can see the CIO reining in the CEOs vision and re-aligning expectations, given the current capabilities of the organization, particularly when they better understand the technical debt and other organizational issues they have to contend with. Building this shared understanding and vision within the c-suite has been described as a "social" dimension of alignment, and defined as the state in which all understand and are committed to the business and IT mission, objectives and plans.[3] In creating a shared understanding of the role of IT in the organization, the CIO will have to build a solid working relationship with peers.

Perhaps not surprising when you reflect on what is being sought, one study found that the frequency of communication between the CIO and the executive team was the strongest indicator of alignment between the strategy of an organization and its portfolio of investments in technology.[4] In essence, it is about having those conversations that matter that we referred to in an earlier chapter. Of course to have these conversations will require a shared language and a common frame of reference. This is the ability of all, at a deep level, to understand and be able to participate in other's key processes and to respect each other's unique contribution and challenges. There must also be a mutual willingness for these conversations to happen in the first instance.

We have noted in an earlier chapter that C-suite colleagues, often have a stereotypical image of the role. It has long been advocated that one important way to overcome this stereotypical image is to "speak the same language" as executive peers. This requires that the CIO has domain knowledge of the business, the industry, competitors and understands priorities and key drivers, and can communicate in a way that does not resort to technical jargon.[5] This is important, as it has been shown that the CIO's domain knowledge of the business in which they work directly impacts the development of shared understanding with their executive colleagues.[6] CIOs who are active members of the executive team will have more frequent formal and informal interactions that build their business knowledge and understanding of key issues and challenges as well as enhancing their credibility.[7] While a self-reinforcing cycle, CIOs need to continually fuel it.

Moreover, CxOs that we spoke to emphasized that knowledge of the business is crucial to the CIO's strategic decision-making authority. This shared domain knowledge also directly influences the CIOs ability to create a common vision for information and technology. Working with the top executive team in this manner also contributes to overcoming the stereotype of the CIO as a "techie." Some CIOs report that they can find themselves in a catch-22 situation: where they struggle to get executive engagement with conversations not happening, leading to a downward spiral that merely reinforces the CIO stereotype.

Peer Stakeholders and Relationships

A factor that was consistently mentioned for a successful CIO transition into a new organization was the strength of their relationships with the other executives on the leadership team. This can be seen from the following quotes:

> First of all, their ability to interact with the rest of the organization and to do it in a way in which they're accepted by the organization. The last thing you want is somebody who comes in who thinks they know it all and they immediately turn off everybody, and they never get that respect back. It doesn't matter how long they're here, because they've set the tone and that becomes the tone by which they're measured going forward. CEO—Diversified Industrial Manufacturer

> It's the emotional intelligence that they show to be able to build relationships. Director-Global Marketing—Food Products Retailer

The importance of peer relationships has been emphasized in other research on executive teams.[8] These aforementioned quotes are consistent with research that shows poor relationships as the dominant cause of executive failure.[9] Executives also shared with us examples of unsuccessful transitions where the CIO did not invest in building relationships.

> I can think of an example where we hired someone in our food service business who went to an operations review. It was 2 weeks after he started, and we'd question why he'd do something a different way, and he'd tell us "you just don't understand, this is the way it needs to be done," and he'd been there only 2 weeks … We were thinking, "well, we see this isn't gonna work." He just wanted to prove what he knew. Frankly after a couple of weeks, we don't expect someone to know what to do … He didn't last that long. CEO—Diversified Industrial Manufacturer

Poor relationships with their executive peers was frequently mentioned as a reason for CIO derailment. This is more than a failure in interpersonal relationships; perhaps an anecdote that we had from a Chief Marketing Officer (CMO) captures this point:

> The CIO proceeded to try to understand all the systems but, the guy fundamentally forgot that there are human beings behind all those processes and all those systems. He totally ignored the relationships, the informal mechanisms, the informal systems.

There are several characteristics that make up good, healthy working relationships:

- *Trust.* This is the foundation of every good relationship. When present, there is a powerful bond with colleagues that helps you to work and communicate more effectively with them. Moreover, if you trust the people you work with, you can be open and honest in your thoughts and actions, and you don't have to waste time and energy "watching your back."
- *Mutual respect.* With mutual respect, you value the input and ideas of colleagues and they value yours. Working together, you can co-create solutions based on your collective insight, wisdom and creativity.
- *Self-aware.* In Chap. 3 we talked about this being a critical trait of successful leaders. Those who are self-aware are careful and attentive to what they say, and they don't let their own negative emotions impact the people around them.
- *Welcoming diversity.* People with good relationships not only accept diverse people and opinions but they welcome them as well. For instance, when colleagues offer different opinions, take the time to consider what they have to say, and factor their insights into your decision-making.
- *Open communication.* The better and more effectively you communicate with those around you, the richer your relationship is likely to be. All good relationships depend on open, honest communication.

Yet, there are subtle elements at work in building relationships with peers. In particular, we found that non-IT executives' perspectives of *their* role in building relationships and working with a CIO vary. Our research data shows that the newly appointed CIO will likely interact with different executives in ways that vary based on the interaction styles and focus of these executives. These dimensions suggest four different types of executive that a CIO is likely to encounter and this taxonomy is shown in Fig. 8.1.

The dimension of *interaction style* indicates whether the executive is passive or active regarding their interacting intension with the CIO. A passive style is one where the executive expects the CIO to take the initiative in the relation-

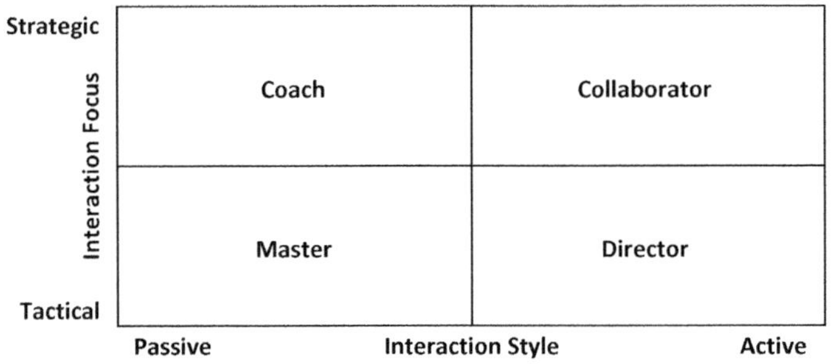

Fig. 8.1 Stakeholder matrix: Interaction focus and style. (Source: Based on A.B. Gerth and J. Peppard, 'The dynamics of CIO derailment: How CIOs come undone and how to avoid it.' *Business Horizons*, Vol. 59, No. 1, pp. 61–70)

ship building process. The "passive" non-IT executive will not initiate a meeting with a newly appointed CIO; rather, he/she will expect the CIO to instead schedule the meeting. Moreover, the passive executive does not view a relationship with the CIO as a high priority. In contrast, the active executives take the initiative in connecting with the CIO. Non-IT executives with an active interaction style view a relationship with the CIO as in their best interest and will be proactive in developing that relationship.

The *interaction focus* can be either tactical or strategic. A tactical focus centers on IT services that the IT organization (and by extension the CIO) provides and requirements that need to be fulfilled. Executives with a tactical interaction focus are concerned with services and new investments for their area of responsibility, but generally do not expect much of a strategic contribution from the CIO (although what they request might be to support strategic initiatives). In contrast, executives with a strategic focus for their interaction expect the CIO to contribute to generating business value with IT and influencing the organization's strategy.

Using this framework, we can identify four types of executive that a CIO might encounter: Master, Director, Coach and Collaborator.

The *Master* has a tactical focus and a passive interaction style. They view the CIO as a technical service provider and the head of a support function. They do not expect the CIO to contribute much to strategic business problem-solving or planning. The Master executive does not initiate interaction with the CIO, but rather expects the CIO to be proactive. The interaction essentially consists of the executive communicating their requirements to the CIO or their representative so that they can be fulfilled. With a delivery focus, unless probed, the Master executive will not voluntarily offer advice on the political power structure or insights on the organization's culture.

The *Director* has a tactical focus but takes an active approach to interacting with the CIO. They will take the initiative to schedule meetings with the CIO on a regular basis. However, the focus will be on the tactical issues of services provided to the executive's function as well as advancing the executive's IT "wish list". Proactively engaging the CIO is viewed by this executive as a politically shrewd way to get their priorities to the top of the CIO's agenda. Similar to the Master, this executive will usually not voluntarily offer advice or insight on organization politics or culture.

While the *Coach* is an executive with a passive interaction style they do focus more on the strategic input of the CIO. This is an executive that will support the CIO if the CIO takes the initiative. While they appreciate that the CIO can contribute to providing business solutions that enable strategy, they still do not view the role as CxO peer. They are willing to work with the CIO and provide them insights into the organization's power structure and any unique cultural aspects they should be aware of.

Finally, the *Collaborator* takes an active approach to engaging the CIO on strategic issues. Taking the initiative to engage the newly appointed CIO, they view the role as a peer on the executive leadership team and recognize the contribution the CIO (and consequently information and technology) can make to innovation and shaping strategic thrusts. In fact, they expect the CIO to make such contributions. They view this active collaboration as a normal part of their role just as they would with any of their operating executive peers.

In a leadership team, CIOs can encounter all four types. If the CIO does not tailor their relationship building activities to the type of executive with whom they are dealing, it can create tension between the two executives. Success at relationships is a function of understanding the other's perspective and meeting them "where they are." Failure to do this can result in poor working relationships and possibly a transition out of the organization. Successful relationships with peers will also increase the CIO's influence, which can be crucial is getting support for commitment for ideas and initiatives.[10]

Peer Influence

Almost every initiative led or proposed by the CIO will require the involvement of his/her executive-suite peers. This means that a CIO cannot rely simply on formal authority to get things done but will demand influencing colleagues, convincing them of efficacy of their proposals and getting them on board to support any proposal or initiative. Successful relationships with peers translate into influence for the CIO. CIOs can then use this influence to gain commitment, involvement and resources to implement new initiatives that will have an impact on the organization.[11]

There are 11 influence techniques commonly used by executives.[12] They are as follows and described in terms of how a CIO might use them to influence a peer:

Apprising: when the CIO explains how the colleague will benefit personally, such as advancing their career.
Coalition: when the CIO seeks the support of others to persuade a colleague, who is perhaps not convinced or hesitating, or the CIO uses this support as a reason the colleague should agree.
Collaboration: when the CIO offers relevant resources and support if the peer will agree to a request.
Consultation: when peer participation and input is sought in order to gain support, such as for planning, implementation or maintaining on-going changes.

Exchange: when favors are traded in return for a colleague's support.

Ingratiation: using flattery, praise or friendliness to convince a colleague to be receptive to the request.

Inspirational appeal: when the CIO couches the request in emotional terms and links it to the organization's vision, values or strategy or their personal goals.

Legitimating: attempting to connect the initiative to precedent, firm policies or role expectations.

Personal appeal: leveraging a colleague's feelings of loyalty and friendship.

Pressure: using demands or persistent reminders to persuade the peer.

Rational persuasion: presenting logical arguments and evidence to persuade a peer.

We can apply these insights into how CIOs use influence techniques to our stakeholder matrix and suggest which techniques are likely be most effective with certain executive types. There are also certain types of influence techniques to avoid using. These recommendations are shown in Table 8.1.

Tailoring the influence technique to the type of executive encountered will help the CIO effectively gain support for a variety of IT initiatives. CIOs should consider several different techniques for each type of executive and avoid those techniques that have a low probability of success or, worse, will result in a weakened relationship.

Table 8.1 Influence technique recommendations for each CxO type

CxO Type	Technique(s) to employ	Technique(s) to avoid
Master	Rational persuasion Apprising Exchange	Pressure Personal appeal Inspirational appeal
Director	Rational persuasion Consultation Apprising Exchange	Pressure Personal appeal Inspirational appeal
Coach	Consultation Collaboration Rational persuasion Apprising Coalition	Pressure Inspirational appeal Personal appeal Ingratiation
Collaborator	Rational persuasion Inspirational appeal Collaboration Coalition Personal appeal	Pressure Ingratiation Legitimating

Source: Authors

Getting Attention for Ideas and Innovation

While technology may provide 'game changer' opportunities, it is often a challenge for the CIO to get attention for them, particularly if the idea or innovation is seen as emanates from within the ranks of the IT unit. This is often compounded if the CIO is relatively new into the organization. Reasons for this include the difficulty in getting engagement, as executives are too busy; weak relationships; the idea is seen as too risky or a reluctance of executives to engage with ideas that challenge deep-seated assumptions and might change the 'status quo; and the lack of credibility of the IT unit to deliver what is required to realize the idea, particularly in Turnaround situations.

One word, perhaps more than most, captures the challenge of getting executive attention: the proposed innovation lacks "legitimacy". So, while an idea might be very relevant and offer significant opportunities, it can still fail to gain any attention in the C-suite. CIOs frequently told us of occasions where proposals they made failed to get much traction, simply because they did not have legitimacy. In some cases, the same ideas were subsequently exploited by a competitor. Achieving legitimacy for an idea, no matter how good it may be, can be a challenge.[13] What drives legitimacy is the credibility of the person promoting the idea, timing and the understanding of the audience of the innovation and its impact.

One CIO told us the story of how he had been hired by a global medical distribution company. His previous background in supply chain and logistics management and his proven success in previous organizations was one of the reasons that he was hired, as this new company had a history of supply chain "glitches". Not long into his new role, he made a presentation to the executive leadership team about how they could streamline key areas of their product distribution process, with the innovative deployment of RFID tags, mobile technologies and redesign of aspects of the logistics process. While he considered it was a "no brainer", he failed to convince the executive team, particularly the CEO, of the validity of the idea and its potential.

One morning, about four months later, the CEO stopped by his office, reminded him of his earlier proposal and suggested that he begin a pilot as he had recently been giving some consideration to his idea and thought that it was now right for the company. He also announced that he would sponsor the pilot. Later that day, the CIO found out that the previous evening the CEO had had dinner with their biggest customer who suggested the same idea the CIO had raised all those months earlier. The CIO's reasoning? The idea now had legitimacy and this legitimacy had been given by the customer.

The CIO reflected that perhaps in presenting his original proposal he lacked credibility, as he was new into the organization and had not yet built up sufficient levels of trust; there was also a history of failed IT investments in the organization prior to him joining. He believed the idea may have had "legs" if it had been presented by someone from the business area that was likely to see the major performance improvement. He also mused that perhaps he had not explained it in a way that his audience understood the innovation and opportunity. Maybe his timing was just off and the executive team were preoccupied with what they considered more pressing issues.

A CIO at law firm told us that if he had a really difficult business case for a technology solution that he really wanted to implement, all he had to say was that one of their competitors was about to deploy the same technology. Another CIO we spoke to mentioned that one board member would always ask "what does Gartner say about this?" when an IT investment proposal came for discussion or approval.[14] As she was always expecting this question, she had a prepared answer, which then gave the proposal added legitimacy. Whatever the reason, without this legitimacy, getting executive attention can prove difficult if not impossible.[15]

Sometimes a prototype, pilot or other form of proof-of-concept can be necessary to give the idea greater credibility. Pushing an idea by creating trusting relationships, understanding the objections and the audience, working toward a win/win situation and using emotion as well as facts to sell the ideas can all help ideas get attention.

Gaining Legitimacy for Ideas

There are a number of possible ways to gain legitimacy for ideas, and these are listed below. These suggestions resonate with research that emphasizes the importance of the social dimension (e.g. shared language, common systems of knowing and trust) in achieving alignment between CIO and their peers.

Build the Trust of Those Who Are Likely to Be Affected Generally, what this means is that they need to know you and feel that you have the best interests of all stakeholders—most especially themselves—at heart. This is the slow part. In most cases, you need to spend time when formulating your ideas, talking to those who are or will be affected; listening to their suggestions, exchanging thoughts, getting to know and trust each other. When open to stakeholders' input, CIOs can create trust and often develop partners who will support you when it comes time to make the final proposal.

Be Honest About Upsides and Downsides How many times have you seen someone lose out on persuading decision makers because they downplayed or did not address the downsides? Either they were so wrapped up in the passion they felt about their proposal that they could not see the negatives (or they were just plain dishonest). Everything has a downside, and the decision makers know that. Make sure you know what it is and be honest about the efforts it will take to overcome these obstacles.

Understand Your Audience Well Audiences are more likely to be interested in the facts of a proposal—how long it will take, what it will cost, what resources will be needed—than how important you think something is, or how passionate you are about it. Other audiences may want something else, and it will be important to understand what that is and to feature it prominently in your arguments.

Work Toward Win/Win You'll never make everyone happy, but you can minimize the damage or negative reactions from the stakeholders who are most affected by what you're proposing and still remain honest about the hurdles.

Use More Than Information Information and facts are very important in presenting ideas. However, influence is most effective when you use compelling language and show your beliefs about what you're proposing in a way that is emotionally expressive. If your audience can see your excitement, they are more likely to approve of what you are proposing.

Building Social Capital

When the CIO of a European government agency took on the role, he was keenly aware that the tenures of previous incumbents had been short lived. He was equally mindful that the IT department he would now lead had a bruising relationship with the rest of the agency. However, he also saw the upside and the tremendous opportunity that digital technologies could bring to the 22,000-person agency, responsible for providing services to that country's unemployed population including making social security payments and helping them find a new job.

But he also knew that he and the IT department could not go it alone if this opportunity was to become a reality. Collaboration and active engagement across all levels of the organization would be mandatory. But to do so would demand tremendous changes, particularly in getting employees from all areas of the business to work together in a productive fashion. This would require more than just creating agile teams or building collaborative platforms. But first, he would have to build relationships with his peers in the C-suite.

During his first six months, he proactively met with and listened to his C-suite colleagues and then went about attending to their problems and concerns. Fortunately for him, all five of Director Generals (equivalent to divisional CEOs and running organizations ranging in size from 1200 to 6000 employees) had huge issues with some of their IT projects and service. So, over his first year, he looked to solve these issues with them. His objective? To build trust and credibility. He also used the opportunity to increase the visibility of IT, demonstrate its capability and begin the process of changing the frame of reference of his c-suite colleagues. To some extent he was lucky that members of the leadership team all recognized that technology could play a much larger role than it was, but were constrained by both their FoR and lack of confidence in the IT unit's ability to deliver. He knew that changing both of these would be vital if he was to achieve his more ambitious vision.

This CIO's story is about a leader who actively strived to build a resource that would provide the foundation for him to push an ambitious digital agenda. His approach is similar to those of other CIOs we've spoken with. These CIOs all shared similar ingredients for their recipe for success in the role, yet none were able to put a specific label on what it was that they were doing. Many of them referred to it as simply networking or building relationships.[16] We have found the concept of social capital describes very well what these CIOs were building. With its origins in economics and sociology, social capital provides a useful integrating framework for configuring and structuring the wide range of activities that these CIOs had instigated and the outcomes that had been achieved. It also aligns very closely with the three phases of taking charge that we have described in the book.

Social capital can be seen as networks of strong, personal relationships developed over time, across functions, groups, units and geographies, which provide the basis for trust, cooperation and collective action.[17] It is built on the notion that the collective abilities of individuals are derived from social networks—the connections or ties that people have; without them, harnessing their combined abilities just won't happen. The central proposition is that this network of relationships constitutes a valuable resource for the conduct for getting things done in an organization; in the case of our CIO, capitalizing on the opportunities that technology offers.

However, having connections or ties to colleagues is a necessary condition but not sufficient to get things done. As we have argued, there also need to be some relational element, such as trust and perhaps values that everybody adheres to. Trust engenders confidence in the CIOs ability to deliver on promises or that the advice being provided is sincere and honest. Another crucial element of social capital is that when people come together, that when they communicate and have conversations, they can understand each other. This will demand a shared frame of reference, or at least to recognize where differences lie.

Social capital is typically unpacked into three interdependent components: structural, cognitive and relational. The structural dimension relates to who you are connected to, both formally and informally. The cognitive dimension refers to conversations and when they happen, that all parties are able to understand each other. Part of the cognitive dimension is that there is a recognition that conversations should take place at all, and this is determined by an executive FoR. The relational dimension is essentially the trust that exist between parties.

The essence of social capital was perhaps best captured by the CIO of the government agency mentioned earlier:

> It has to do with mutual trust and to invest on a, let's say, person to person level. Do we really understand each other? Do we wanna work together? Do we wanna make a success of this difficult task that we have to do together? And if you invest, and let's say you love to do these things together, you can make anything possible. And it has sometimes to do with formal structures and formal decisions, the governances and things like that, but most of the times, it's the ease of finding each other, if you have things to discuss or solve.

To understand the social capital of a CIO requires an analysis of their existing social networks in the organization and the corresponding ties and connections that they have with their peers; the existing shared language, frames of meaning and mechanisms of collective sense-making; and the level of trust and reciprocity between employees. While the structural dimension determines who the CIO is connected to, the latter two are key ingredients in facilitating real value-add conversation, collaboration and the co-creation of shared understanding and of new knowledge, vital for success in the role.

As we can see, social capital is not a unitary concept but is multidimensional and therefore will require a variety of activities and initiatives that will need to be orchestrated. Ultimately, the presence of strong social capital facilitates the kind of conversations that collaboration and engagement across the enterprise seeks. The process of building social capital aligns very well with the three phases of taking charge that we have presented earlier in the book. In Table 8.2, we illustrate the relationship between both.

Table 8.2 Building social capital through the process of taking charge

		Phases of taking charge		
		Entry	**Stabilization**	**Renewal**
Dimensions of social capital	**Structural**	Building connections by meeting with new colleagues Understanding the informal networks	Regular meetings Establish IT governance processes and mechanisms Strategy reviews	Regular meetings Extend network Strategy reviews
	Cognitive	Assess the FoR of colleagues Conversations that matter	Amending the frames of reference Rationale for governance Conversations that matter	Continues with conversations that matter
	Relational	Listening Understand issues and challenges	Deliver on promises Co-create solutions Solicit inputs	Co-create solutions

Source: Authors

Leading CIOs, when they assume the role in a new organization, recognize that they have zero social capital and set about building it in the early weeks and months of their tenure.[18] They proactively reach out to meet new C-suite colleagues to begin the process of building connections and to understand their issues and challenges. They spend a lot of time listening, looking to deliver solutions to their problems to begin building the trust and credibility that is so fundamental to social capital and taking charge. They also recognize that conversations about digital are two-way and look to help their business colleagues become more digitally savvy. As we have argued on many occasions in this book, if colleagues struggle to understand technology or have an inappropriate frame of reference it is unlikely they will be in a position to have any meaningful conversations, and progress will be stilted.

Successful Transitions Are All About People!

This chapter covered two dimensions related to CIOs and relationships with colleagues. Good relationships with their peers are critical to the CIO's success in their role. A newly appointed CIO must recognize that they face pre-existing perceptions of the CIO role and expectations associated with it. Building effective relationships with peers will include understanding these pre-existing perceptions along the continuum that we presented. Understanding the stakeholder's preference for interaction style and focus will also help the CIO tailor influence techniques. Effectively managing the dynamics of stakeholder perceptions, styles and influence techniques will contribute significantly to the newly appointed CIO's success in the organization. Ultimately, the CIO is building the social capital that can be leveraged during their tenure to help in achieving mutually beneficial outcomes.

Notes

1. See D. Preston and E. Karahanna, 'Antecedents of IS strategic alignment: A nomological network', *Information Systems Research*, Vol. 20, 2009, pp. 159–179; D. Smaltz, V. Sambamurthy and R. Agarwal, 'The antecedents of CIO role effectiveness in organizations: An empirical study in the healthcare sector', *IEEE Transactions on Engineering Management*, Vol. 53, 2006, pp. 207–222 and S. Wei and T.S. Cho, 'Exploring involuntary executive turnover through a managerial discretion framework', *Academy of Management Review*, Vol. 30, 2005, pp. 843–854.
2. Some examples of these pre-existing perceptions are discussed by M. Kaarst-Brown, 'Understanding an organization's view of the CIO: The role of assumptions about IT', *MIS Quarterly Executive*, Vol. 4, 2005, pp. 287–301 and P.A. Gonzalez, L. Ashworth and J. McKeen, 'The CIO stereotype: Content, bias, and impact', *The Journal of Strategic Information Systems*, Vol. 28, No. 1, 2019, pp. 83–99.
3. B. Reich and I. Benbasat, 'Factors that influence the social dimension of alignment between business and information technology objectives', *MIS Quarterly*, Vol. 24, 2000, pp. 81–113.
4. B. Reich and I. Benbasat, 'Factors that influence the social dimension of alignment between business and information technology objectives', *MIS Quarterly*, Vol. 24, 2000, pp. 81–113.
5. S. Wei and T.S. Cho, 'Exploring involuntary executive turnover through a managerial discretion framework', *Academy of Management Review*, Vol. 30, 2005, pp. 843–854. See also M. Wiersema and A. Bird, 'Organizational demography in Japanese firms: Group heterogeneity, individual dissimilarity, and top management team turnover', *The Academy of Management Journal*, Vol. 36, 1993, pp. 996–1025.
6. D.S. Preston and E. Karahanna, 'Antecedents of IS strategic alignment: A nomological network', *Information Systems Research*, Vol. 20, 2009, pp. 159–179.
7. B. Reich and I. Benbasat, 'Factors that influence the social dimension of alignment between business and information technology objectives', *MIS Quarterly*, Vol. 24, 2000, pp. 81–113.

8. W. Boeker, 'Executive migration and strategic change: The effect of top manager movement on product-market entry', *Administrative Science Quarterly*, Vol. 42, 1997, pp. 213–236; D. Hambrick and P. Mason, 'Upper echelons: The organization as a reflection of its top managers', *Academy of Management Review*, Vol. 9, 1984, pp. 193–206; W. Shen and A.A. Cannella Jr., 'Power dynamics within top management and their impacts on CEO dismissal followed by inside succession', *Academy of Management Journal*, Vol. 45, 2002, pp. 1195–1206 and M. Wiersema and A. Bird, 'Organizational demography in Japanese firms: Group heterogeneity, individual dissimilarity, and top management team turnover', *Academy of Management Journal*, Vol. 36, 1993, pp. 996–1025.

9. J.F. Manzoni and J.L. Barsoux, 'The interpersonal side of taking charge', *Organizational Dynamics*, Vol. 38, No. 2, 2009, pp. 106–116; J. Gabarro, *The Dynamics of Taking Charge*, Harvard Business School Press, Boston, 1987 and S. Davis, 'Should a 60 percent success rate be acceptable?' *Industrial and Commercial Training*, Vol. 37, No. 7, 2005, pp. 331–335.

10. There is a deep research pool of how a CIO's relationships with the rest of the executive leadership team impacts their effectiveness. A small sample of these studies are D.F. Feeny, B.R. Edwards and K.M. Simpson, 'Understanding the CEO/CIO relationship', *MIS Quarterly*, Vol. 16, No. 4, 1992, pp. 435–448; M. Kaarst-Brown, 'Understanding an organization's view of the CIO: The role of assumptions about IT', *MIS Quarterly Executive*, Vol. 4, 2005, pp. 287–301; D. Preston, D. Leidner, and D. Chen, 'CIO leadership profiles: Implications of matching CIO authority and leadership capability on it impact', *MIS Quarterly Executive*, Vol. 7, 2008, pp. 57–69; J. Peppard, 'Unlocking the performance of the chief information officer (CIO)', *California Management Review*, Vol. 52, 2010, pp. 73–99 and J. Gerow, V. Grover and J. Thatcher, 'Power and politics: Do CIOs have what it takes to influence the executive team's commitment to IT initiatives?' *AMCIS 2012 Proceedings*, Paper 1.

11. See J.A. Conger, 'The necessary art of persuasion', *Harvard Business Review*, May–June, 1998, pp. 84–97.

12. See D. Kipnis, S.M. Schmidt, and I. Wilkinson, 'Intraorganizational influence tactics: Explorations in getting one's way', *Journal of Applied Psychology*, Vol. 65, No. 4, 1980, pp. 440–452; G. Yukl, *Leadership in Organizations* (5th ed.), Prentice-Hall, 2002. The following studies focused solely on CIOs: H. Enns, S. Huff, and C. Higgins, 'CIO lateral influence behaviors: Gaining peers' commitment to strategic information systems', *MIS Quarterly*, Vol. 27, No. 1, 2003, pp. 155–176 and H. Enns and S. Huff, 'How CIOs can effectively use influence behaviors', *MIS Quarterly Executive*, Vol. 6, No. 1, 2007, pp. 29–38.

13. See J. Hall, V. Bachor and S. Matos, 'Developing and diffusing new technologies: Strategies for legitimization', *California Management Review*, Vol. 56, No. 3, 2014, pp. 98–117; B.E. Ashforth and B.W. Gibbs, 'The double-edge

of organizational legitimation', *Organization Science*, Vol. 1, No. 2, 1990, pp. 177–194; R. Suddaby and R. Greenwood, 'Rhetorical strategies of legitimacy', *Administrative Science Quarterly*, Vol. 50, No. 1, 2005, pp. 35–67 and M.C. Suchman, 'Managing legitimacy: Strategic and institutional approaches', *Academy of Management Review*, Vol. 20, No. 3, 1995, pp. 571–610.

14. For a sociological study of the influence of Gartner's 'Magic Quadrant', see N. Pollock and R. Williams, 'The sociology of a market analysis tool: How industry analysts sort vendors and organize markets', *Information and Organization*, Vol. 19, 2009, pp. 129–151.

15. For a study of building legitimacy for IT innovations, see E. Kaganer, S. Pawlowski and S. Wiley-Patton, 'Building legitimacy for IT innovations: The case of computerized physician order entry systems', *Journal of the Association for Information Systems*, Vol. 11, No. 1, 2010, pp. 1–33.

16. For more on how leaders create networks, see H. Ibarra and M. Hunter, 'How leaders create and use networks', *Harvard Business Review*, January, 2007, pp. 40–47.

17. W. Tsai and S. Ghoshal, 'Social capital and value creation: The role of intrafirm networks', *Academy of Management Journal*, Vol. 41, No. 4, 1998, pp. 464–476; P.S. Adler and S.-W. Kwon, 'Social capital: Prospects for a new concept', *Academy of Management Review*, Vol. 27, No. 1, 2002, pp. 17–40; J. Nahapiet and S. Ghoshal, 'Social capital, intellectual capital, and the organizational advantage', *Academy of Management Review*, Vol. 23, 1998, pp. 242–266 and D. Krackhardt and J. R. Hanson, 'Informal networks: The company behind the chart', *Harvard Business Review*, July–August 1993, pp. 104–111.

18. For a study that has looked at the relationship between social capital and CIO-CxO relationships, see E. Karahanna and D. Preston, 'The effect of social capital on the relationship between the CIO and top management team on firm performance', *Journal of Management Information Systems*, Vol. 30, No. 1, 2013, pp. 15–55.

9

Taking Off: Guidance to CIOs

As we mentioned in the beginning of the book, the core objective of our research has been to better understand how CIOs take charge in a new appointment, to identify what makes for a successful CIO transition and to surface how to avoid derailment. However insightful these might be, there should be a "so what?" The "so what" for us is to provide practical guidance to coach CIOs on how to be more effective and ultimately play the role of a leader with special responsibility for information and technology in the organization.

In the era of digital disruption and transformation, the CIO role in organizations has become even more important. To that end, we share ten key recommendations for CIOs to consider when taking on a new appointment that will maximize the probability that they will be successful. These have been distilled from our data. The key recommendations are as follows:

1. Be prepared for surprises, even after extensive due diligence
2. Understand that the Entry phase is primarily about learning
3. Proactively build relationships with peers
4. Don't introduce change too quickly
5. Realize what worked in the past may not be successful again
6. Be clear as to what constitutes success
7. Build a shared vision for the role and contribution of IT
8. Cultivate a Frame of Reference appropriate for success with information and technology
9. Earn the right to influence business strategy
10. There are no shortcuts to taking charge

© The Author(s) 2020
T. Gerth, J. Peppard, *Taking the Reins as CIO*,
https://doi.org/10.1007/978-3-030-31953-3_9

In the remainder of the chapter, we'll expand on each one of these guidelines. The practices that we elude to come straight from the CIOs themselves and provide guidance on actions that will increase the probability of success; unfortunately, they don't guarantee it.

Be Prepared for Surprises, Even After Extensive Due Diligence

All of the CIOs that we talked to performed some degree of due diligence about the potential new role. Sources of information about the organization and its strategy came from the CEO and other top executives. The executive recruiter working for the hiring organization was also a source, however often not an accurate one. There were other sources that our CIOs tapped as well. Suppliers of information technology and consulting services were good sources of "inside" information on politics and where the organization had been with regard to the IT organization and their perspective of the previous leadership. Many of the CIOs had pre-existing relationships with these suppliers from previous roles and therefore were confident in the veracity of the information they provided. Other stakeholders such as customers and board members were also sources of information. Finally, the network of CIOs in professional organizations or other relationships were sounding boards that the executive utilized.

CIOs reported that the situations they encountered when they assumed their roles were generally somewhat different from what they expected. Due diligence does not replace actually being on the ground in the new position. This is not to imply that you will be intentionally misled by either the recruiter or the executives you talk to during the hiring process. A CIO (or any executive) can only fully understand the situation he/she inherits by working within the organization with new colleagues on a daily basis and digging into details difficult to assess during the recruitment process.

This book can help shape your due diligence by trying to identify the dynamics that we have outlined throughout the chapters, especially those directly related to success in a new role. Often the surprises will be positive! Prepare for surprises even if they can be negative and frustrating. Many of our CIOs emphasized that being adaptable is an important characteristic of successful CIOs.

Understand the Entry Phase Is Primarily About Learning

New leaders often feel pressured to "make an impact" in the first 90 days and many management books emphasize that point. Our research suggests taking a slightly more moderate approach. As we've pointed out, in Turnaround transitions often quick action is required to solve service delivery issues or pull a project out of the ditch. We are not advocating you wait if urgency is required. We are suggesting, however, that you use the majority of your "honeymoon" on understanding the organization's strategy, politics, technology strengths and weaknesses and where the biggest challenges and opportunities are.

Use the early weeks and months to learn about the organization. This goes beyond simply identifying IT service problems or assessing the project portfolio or evaluating the legacy technology landscape. It includes understanding the political environment, company culture and strategy, as well as identifying the key influencers and power brokers. You can do a number of things in this phase to gather information.

One-on-One Meetings with Stakeholders and Their Team Members

Meet with your peers on the executive team and find out what their "hot button" issues are regarding how information and technology is enabling their strategy. Ask about their view of the IT organization and solicit suggestions on areas of improvement as well as areas of strength to build upon. If you can, also meet with their direct reports and others who are "in the trenches" to assess how the applications that support them and data are regarded. Meet with key customers to find out what their customer experience is like when engaging with the organization. If appropriate, a selection of ecosystem partners should also be visited.

Group Discussions with Functions/Departments/ Geographies

When one-on-one meetings are not efficient or possible consider conducting focus group sessions with the same questions as the one-on-one meetings described above. Remember the group dynamics aspect might bias the information you receive, but the information may still be valuable. Conduct virtual meetings with far flung entities if necessary. Just remember that the personal touch is more impactful coming from a new executive. You should make it a priority to meet people in person.

Meet with Your Own Team, Individually and in Groups

Gather information from your own team as well, starting with your direct reports. It is critical to understand their experience, concerns and solicit their input on changes that you are considering. This is a way of building buy-in and gaining useful information about the politics in play between the IT unit and stakeholders. Remember this information will likely be biased as you assess your action plan. It is equally important to communicate with all members of your IT organization, not just the senior leadership team. This is your new team and it is important to begin building a rapport with them. One warning: you might be tempted to jump to an articulation of the future in order to set a positive tone. Wait until you have collected all the information you need and have had time to reflect upon it. Don't give into the temptation of making commitments too soon.

Review Plans, Standards, Policies and Other Strategic Documents

Reviewing documents is tedious, but a valuable opportunity to see what is written down and what is not. Is there a formal set of technology standards? A formal architecture? What does the information and technology (and/or digital) strategy look like, assuming there is one? Trace along some customer journeys to understand touchpoints that are dependent on technology. This review will give you the opportunity to identify areas where more formal documentation is required. It will provide insight into possible gaps between what actually goes on in the organization (reality) and what is written down (theory). You can also assess the quality of the thinking that went into the documents and plans and, by extension, gain insight into the quality of the people writing them.

Assess the Program Status of the Largest IT Initiatives

Inflight projects might be a significant risk to the organization, so you want to review these in your first 90 days. Not every project needs to be reviewed. Focus your attention on projects and programs based on the following criteria:

- Projects that impact your key stakeholders, especially those they mentioned in your one-on-one meetings
- Projects that have a significant impact on the operational infrastructure of the organization, its technology, security and data.
- Projects with significant budgets and/or risk to business operations
- Projects focused on improving customer experience.

This review should include project- and service-specific interviews (e.g. with project managers, service managers and business owners) as well as reviewing project documentation, at least at a summary level. There are many project management/risk management frameworks that you can use to provide a cursory understanding of the project's status. Do not rely solely on the formal project status reports. These often are overly optimistic by design and do not always provide a clear understanding of the *real* status. You need confidence that a project is under control otherwise it probably needs remediation. Projects in need of remediation will usually need some immediate action. This review also will provide information on the maturity of the program management capability of the organization as a whole and your team specifically.

Assess Your Leadership Team's Current Capabilities and Potential to Lead in the Future

The importance of the CIOs own leadership team was emphasized by every CIO and is a critical factor in building credibility. After you have met with stakeholders, your team, reviewed documentation and assessed key projects, you will have sufficient information to make judgments about your senior leadership team. You will also be able to make credible statements to them about their performance based on your own assessment and not merely organizational hearsay. It's important to assess both their current performance in current roles, whether a different role is a better fit and whether the person has the future potential to lead consistent with your vision of for information, technology and the IT unit. Your conclusion will boil down to these options for each individual:

- Retain—high potential—priority to retain
- Retain—keeper—retain if possible
- Redeploy inside of IT—keeper that is simply in the wrong role
- Redeploy outside of IT—person who is wrong for an IT role but might benefit another function
- Release—release this person from the organization.

You can also review the performance documentation of others in the organization to gain knowledge of where individuals might be that can step up into new roles as well. After this assessment, you can work with the HR function to develop retention, redeployment and release plans as needed.

Observe the Power Dynamics in Meetings That You Attend

Observation as an information gathering technique is as important as talking to stakeholders and your team. How people behave in meetings can be very insightful as to your stakeholder analysis and how to work with them. Do they challenge assumptions and demand evidence? Do they respond to peer pressure? Do they dominate the conversation or do they facilitate it? Does a person's actions conflict with their words and commitments? Are they consistent? Are they perceived as a leader among peers? All of these observations will help you understand the informal systems and organizational politics that are the foundation for effective relationship building and exerting influence.

Even if you are promoted as an insider it is critical that you approach this phase as an outsider would. While insiders know some of the information above, they are usually insulated from many of the dynamics faced by the CIO in terms of enterprise-wide priorities.

Proactively Build Relationships with Peers

As you have seen, we interviewed the executive suite peers of CIOs, which confirmed that many of them expect CIOs to proactively approach them for information, engagement and relationship building; it is unlikely that all will take the initiative to connect with a new CIO. As well as doing the normal tour of stakeholders in the first few months, new CIOs must carry out a detailed stakeholder analysis. They need to identify who are IT advocates and who are adversaries or, at best, skeptics. They should ask direct questions that elicit information about the decision-making culture and priority-setting. Identify and understand the executives with the most strategic business initiatives and target them for support. The framework provided in the previous chapter is a good starting point for this analysis.

The quality of the peer relationships held by CIOs is a critical factor in their success. The best approach is to be proactive with all stakeholders in having regular interactions. Focus on adding value during each conversation. A new CIO needs to expect that relationships will develop and grow at different paces with different stakeholders. Not all of your peers will be as receptive as others to your overtures. Meet them where they are and use stakeholder analysis to focus your attention on the most valuable stakeholders without starving the others for attention.

Remember that relationships require trust and trust requires time: this is why social capital takes so long to build. A CIO shared that it took more than 90 days before people really opened up to him as opposed to giving the politically correct information. You may be fortunate and find some quick allies to get started. Most of the relationships that you build will take more time to ferment. While stakeholder analysis is worthwhile, don't underestimate the value of delivering on commitments like inflight projects and resolving any service delivery issues. You can win many hearts and minds by initially delivering excellent service to the organization. This gives them confidence in you.

Don't Introduce Change Too Quickly

A new CIO may be eager to make an impact, but the evidence suggests that he or she should not be in too much of a hurry to make changes. Obviously, in a Turnaround transition, a new CIO may be forced to take corrective action immediately after taking up the role, often without a rigorous assessment or complete knowledge. Severe service delivery issues also must take priority. However, in most transitions, too much change too fast will damage credibility and send a message to other executives that the CIO is not trying to fit into the organization by learning before acting.

The danger is to push change too fast and be viewed as insensitive and disruptive. Alternatively, introducing change too slowly may be interpreted as a lack of initiative. In the entry phase, it is important to understand "how things are done" and the organization's capacity for change. The go-forward action plan should include a "culturally appropriate" pace of change. One CIO described better than we could: *"If you are a sprinter and come into a walking organization then you are going to have to walk. I have to slow down on most things and maybe just press for one large change at a time."*

Realize What Worked in the Past May Not Be Successful Again

Successful transitions were described as "doing the right things (i.e. getting results), the right way (i.e. fitting the culture)." A new CIO cannot assume that what worked in a previous organization will be successful in the current environment. This concept is explained in great detail in Marshall Goldsmith's popular leadership book entitled "*What Got You Here Won't Get You There*".[1] In his book, he focuses on the 20 habits that hold executives back. CIOs did not report such habits to us per se, but they did articulate a similar theme that what they did at previous organizations would not necessarily work in the present one.

It is easy to assume you know the answers if you have been successful in the past. CIOs generally have a lot of past success and they apply that experience throughout their career. The caveat here, as reported through our data, is to temper that inclination until you have clearly understood the uniqueness of the new organizational context. This understanding comes mainly from information gathering in the Entry phase.

Be Clear as to What Constitutes Success

The notion of success can be very subjective; what the CIO interprets as success might be at odds with that of the CEO and the C-suite. Earlier we discussed the gap between CIOs' perspective of success and what many non-IT executives view as success criteria for IT initiatives. The new CIO needs to identify the definition of success early on and then manage expectations accordingly. This definition of success should also be "baked" into the project management approach for any initiative to ensure that success criteria are met. In the beginning, it is less important what the success criteria are than that all stakeholders have a shared understanding of them. However, depending on the frame of reference for what success entails, amending this may need focus. Our research showed that most non-IT executives view success criteria for investments in IT very narrowly as budget, schedule and/or functionality. While there is strong evidence that business benefits are the best way to prove that IT investments are successful, this might be a battle for another day for the new CIO! The critical thing here is that the project meets whatever success criteria have been jointly agreed upon so that the initiative is viewed widely as successful.

Managing success criteria with peers will also contribute to the positive perception of delivering on commitments. As one CIO put it: *"never, ever, ever promise something you do not already know you can deliver. Otherwise, your credibility goes right into the shredder! You don't promise anything that you don't already know is a fact!"*

Build a Shared Vision for the Role and Contribution of IT

CIO success will ultimately be determined by the extent to which the direction for information and technology is driven by the CIO and a shared vision for these in the organization is built. Being forward-looking—envisioning exciting possibilities and enlisting others in a shared view of the future—is the attribute that most distinguishes leaders. Digital transformation provides the perfect opportunity for the CIO to establish a customer focused, value-driven vision.

Creating this shared vision will accomplish several things are critical to the CIO's success. It will ensure that the CIO and CEO and other top executives are on the same page as to the role that the IT organization should play. This can be mapped to our previous discussion as to how the CIO is viewed as Service Provider, Solutions Provider or Strategic Contributor. This shared vision among the executive team will provide legitimacy for the CIO as the IT leader and create a foundation on which to build into a business leader role. A shared vision will include success criteria that everyone agrees upon. Finally, a shared vision also results in an IT unit that is excited about its role in the business and how IT contributes to business success. This leads to retention of key talent and act as a magnet attracting talent into the organization.

Cultivate a Frame of Reference Appropriate for Success with Information and Technology

Brown bag lunches, seminars and workshops can be worthwhile in educating top executives in the potential of information and IT, but don't expect these activities alone to increase the IT-savvy of executive stakeholders. Often, the best way to achieve this is to demonstrate that IT can generate value and enable key business strategies. This requires setting realistic expectations before commencing any project, getting stakeholder buy-in and commitment for required organizational changes, ensuring effective delivery of the project and expected benefits and measuring and communicating results post-implementation. Success can be used as an example to others in the organization and can build momentum for change.

Remember, not all executives will have bought into the shared responsibility view of IT and will see anything to do with information and IT as falling outside the scope of their responsibilities. Seek out executives "who get IT" and look to them to provide strong IT advocacy. A CIO described it well *"IT used to be a service provider and order taker and expectations were low. Now we've transformed IT and more people ask 'hey can you help us here, why can't we move any faster'."*

Earn the Right to Influence Business Strategy

A new CIO needs to build credibility as an effective leader of the IT organization before he/she can influence top management peers and the business strategy. Many business executives are likely to withhold support until the CIO's credibility has been established. Remember, credibility has to be earned by effectively delivering and improving IT services, by successfully completing in-flight projects and demonstrating business benefits and by building an IT leadership team that evokes confidence in their peers. Only then will the CIO gain the legitimacy needed to influence more strategic business decisions.

This dichotomy has been described as supply-side leadership and demand-side leadership.[2] Supply-side leadership describes the service delivery and project management aspects of the CIO's role, the domain of the leader of an IT organization. Demand-side leadership describes how the CIO plays a strategic role in co-evolving IT strategy with the other executive team members. There is research that confirms that playing a strategic influence (demand-side leadership) is dependent on effective leadership of the IT organization (supply-side).[3] Strategic legitimacy takes time and a new CIO must build that credibility with their peers.

There Are No Shortcuts to Successfully Taking Charge

A 90-day plan, as advocated in popular books, is all well and good, but a new CIO should recognize that a plan for the next two years and beyond will also be needed. The early weeks and months should primarily be about learning. Don't assume that what happens in the first 90 days is all that matters! The first 90–100 days is an important first step, but there are two other phases, Stabilization and Renewal, that ultimately determine the CIO's success. Working through these phases takes approximately two years so a longer-term plan needs to evolve after the CIO engages in their initial entry phase. Advice from one of our CIO interviewees, unprompted, was *"do not drink the Kool-Aid and believe that you can be successful as CIO by reading the 90-day plan checklist in a book somewhere"*.

Transition type influences the intensity of the changes that may be required. Turnaround transitions certainly require more intensive and immediate actions than Success-sustaining transitions (e.g. major changes in the IT leadership team vs. very minor changes). However, regardless of transition type, a new CIO will experience the three phases and timelines discussed earlier. Taking charge, even in a Success-sustaining transition, will still take two years or more; there is still the need to build confidence, credibility and legitimacy. There are no shortcuts to effective leadership in a CIO role.

Good Luck!

These guidelines are insights that have come from our research and have been covered earlier in various chapters. We summarize them here as a quick reference. Like any "best practices" list these actions do not guarantee success but, rather, increase the likelihood of success. It is almost certain that if you do not do at least these ten things that you will not be successful.[4] The CIO role is complex and high risk. The advent of the digital revolution and transformation of many organizations have made the CIO role more important than ever. The nature of the role and the career opportunities for successful CIOs mean that there is often a high voluntary turnover of CIOs within and across industries. This signals that many CIOs every year are entering new appointments and transitioning into new organizations. Other IT leaders are being promoted into the CIO role and facing new leadership challenges. The cost of failure is high to both the organization and to the CIO.[5]

Our objective in conducting this research and writing this book has been to provide CIOs a robust, evidence-based set of actions to consider in order to increase their probability of success. Some of these actions might be perceived as "management common-sense", but the failure rate of CIOs and the persistent gap in the C-suite's understanding of information and IT indicate that this is not common sense at all. In fact, it is more common that many of these dynamics are ignored than implemented. We hope we have accomplished our goal and that these insights will be helpful. The successful digital transformation of every organization depends on a strategic and successful Chief Information Officer.

Notes

1. M. Goldsmith, *What Got You Here Won't Get You There: How Successful People Become Even More Successful*, Profile Books, 2010.
2. M. Broadbent and E. Kitzis, *The New CIO Leader: Setting the Agenda and Delivering Results*, Harvard Business School Press, Boston 2005.

3. An academic paper that is very quantitative but delivers insights is D. Preston, D. Chen and D. Leidner, 'Examining the antecedents and consequences of CIO strategic decision-making authority: An empirical study', *Decision Sciences*, Vol. 39, 2008, pp. 605–642.
4. A.B. Gerth and J. Peppard, 'The dynamics of CIO derailment: How CIOs come undone and how to avoid it', *Business Horizons*, Vol. 59, No. 1, 2016, pp. 61–70.
5. Ibid.

10

Advice from CIOs to CIOs

The guidance provided in this book is essentially the result of patterns that we have observed from our interviews with CIOs, CxO, analysts, academics and recruiters as we explored with them the taking charge process. In our narrative, we have shared stories and insights from CIOs themselves. While many of these have been recounted in their actual words, their voices have been anonymous. We thought it would be appropriate to wrap up the book with advice directly from named CIOs. We invited them to share their answer to a simple question; "what advice would you give a CIO on taking up a new appointment?" They are all accomplished executives with deep experiences as a Chief Information Officer. These are their words, edited only for length, not context nor content.

Karen Alber (Former CIO of MillerCoors, HJ Heinz)[1]

My first piece of advice would be to make sure that you're honest as to what your skillset is and that you understand what they're looking for. If they're looking for a super technical leader and you're a very strategic leader it's going to be a pretty tough row to hoe once you get in-house. I think you really have to be honest about what the company is trying to achieve and are you the right skill set for the role. You might really want the job, but you'll immediately know you're not a fit.

It's my favorite coaching to give if you're moving into the CIO job and even if you've been in the company already, I still advise that you act like an

© The Author(s) 2020
T. Gerth, J. Peppard, *Taking the Reins as CIO*,
https://doi.org/10.1007/978-3-030-31953-3_10

outsider. Then you restart the listening and learning process because you're now doing it from a different lens. You're going to have the natural instinct to want to drive change and make a stamp right away. My advice is to fight that instinct and make sure that you listen and learn in those first 90 days. Learn the business and understand what their goals are and what the business is all about. Then you will have some confidence that you know the business. My three big words for the first 90 days would be relationships, relationships, relationships. I believe that the CIO job is a people job not just a technical job. Technical skills are important, but they really are just table stakes.

You usually inherit a team. Go to school on your team and meet as many people as you can. In the first six months, I make an effort to meet and talk with every single employee in the organization one-on-one. Make sure you get to understand not only the people but also the organizational structure. I walked into one organization that had a traditional IT structure which was fine for the previous five years, but for the next five, we needed to look at how to move projects through a more process-oriented and transformative IT organization. Once you have made an assessment of the talent, you'll need to be willing to make the hard calls because you can't do these jobs without having the right team around you. You don't have a long time to do that. The business isn't going to give you a free four years! Usually, they'll give you those first few months to learn and after that you have to start moving the needle.

Within the first 120 days, I told the company leadership team that I would do a state of the business review with them after I had a chance to assess the situation. This organization was having a pretty tough time with some systems and IT's overall lack of credibility. So, I put together a well-thought-out "what's working/what's not working" both on how we supported the business and what we need to do. I went into that leadership team meeting to inform the group that we didn't have an IT problem we had a business problem and it resonated with many leaders in the room. Basically, what I said is "hey I can fix some of this within my own shop, some of it is just blocking and tackling, but a large part of it is how we as a company use IT."

I ask people to tell me what you remember about the most impactful CIO or leader in general that you ever worked for. They describe to me how the CIO had their back, was supportive and let us make mistakes and understood how to handle failure. They always describe leadership qualities, not technical skills. You're going to have to make a decision pretty early on as to what do you want to be known for. Do you want to be known for being a great technical advisor or do you want to be known for being a transformative leader? You want to be known for helping grow the business.

Dr. Michael Müller-Wünsch (CIO Otto; Formerly SVP Corporate IT [CIO] of Lekkerland AG & Co.KG; Partner at HiSolutions AG; Various Roles CEVA Logistics; Chief Operating Officer of myToys.de)[2]

I am acutely aware that when a company brings in a new CIO, it is often expecting miracles and with no budget! So, for me, your first task should be to establish expectations. I recommend engaging with the supervisory board[3] or any superior executive structure to get a sense as to how they will judge whether you are successful or not. What are the metrics, the quantitative and qualitative measures they will use to determine if you have succeeded? This will also help enormously in framing your initial agenda, particularly in identifying key areas where you should give attention to as you begin the process of understanding the company, its strategy, competitors, customers, culture and so on. Knowing expectations will help you in managing them. So if the board expect that you will refresh the applications landscape, and you estimate that it will cost 20 million euro to do so but they are only giving you a budget of 5 million euro, then it is unlikely that you will make the great leap forward.

For any newly appointed CIO, in the early months, I would recommend focusing on what I call "The Double T": Trust and Transparency.

If you are going to be successful as a CIO, it is imperative that you establish a trusting and meaningful relationship with all your key stakeholders. I suggest initially seeing them as two "teams." Your first team of stakeholders will be the Board and the senior executive committee. The second will be your own tech community. CIOs have a tendency to spend most of their time with the latter team. If your assumption on taking the role is that you will sit in your ivory tower, you won't last very long. You will need to forge good productive relationships with the first team if you want to have influence and be that business enabler and not seen as an IT service provider, in the sense of a supplier rather than a true business partner.

During your first few months, work on getting to know each member of the executive team. Schedule regular meetings with them to understand their drivers, challenges and issues. Trust is ultimately gained by delivering, so I would suggest identifying a pain point in the organization and focus on solving that. Look for something where you can deliver a tangible result—not something that lies "under the carpet" and is invisible. This might be a new business functionality that helps procurement or a new feature that will delight customers. Then you need to be exact: "I promise to deliver, within 4 months, within budget and within scope, these specific benefits and business outcomes."

It is imperative that you stick to any promises you make. Make sure that you have your IT team behind you and that they also believe it is achievable and are fully committed. Delivering on your promises impacts your credibility. When you deliver promises, you can then start thinking about big projects and more strategic initiatives which are likely to be riskier. Remember, you don't do this in your ivory tower; get out and constantly engage with your colleagues from the business side.

You will also need to have full transparency of your new tech organization, particularly the costs and the organization performance. Look at all expenditures so that you have a clear understanding of the IT cost structure. How much of the spend, for example, is accounted for by depreciation? Try to determine what is the moveable, by that I mean money that is already committed but could potentially be shifted and used for other purposes. Talk to your leadership team, especially the enterprise architects, to understand the technical debt that you have inherited and its implications. I suggest doing this application by application so that you can make an assessment of how long the application is in place and for how long was it planned to be operational. Try to get a sense as to whether these are capable of meeting future functional and non-functional demands. With your team, calculate the financial implications of any technical debt.

While these early months are concerned with you gaining transparency around your IT organization and the technology landscape you should also be looking to eventually providing this same transparency to your stakeholders. This will also help in fueling the trusting relationships that are so important as well as help you in managing expectations.

Sometimes you will encounter peers who do not quite understand the role of data and technology in a modern enterprise. Very often, their understanding is derived from what they have heard about tech costs, that it could be spent more efficiently and, by default, that the problem is the CIOs. You will need to actively work with these colleagues, particularly if they are influential, to change their perspective if you are going to get the engagement and involvement that you will ultimately need.

Demonstrate to them the tradeoff between automation, that is, between tech and people. I sometimes "propose" that I could immediately eliminate all tech costs by shutting down all servers, networks and applications. This usually focuses their attention on the value side of the equation! Invite them to make a joint analysis of what is beneficial for the organization. Explain how to employ tech to generate business benefits and that success will be a joint effort. In exploring the implications of technical debt, I like to use the analogy of architecture. If you have a Venetian palace, it is unlikely that you will have an environmentally friendly usage of that building. Its upkeep will be costly, as it's not as efficient compared to modern buildings. It also lacks the functionality required for today's modern living. Sometimes it can take well over a year to get everybody on the same page so that you no longer talk about absolute costs in technology discussions.

As you talk to your colleagues on the business side, you will quickly see that they would like to have everything faster, more agile, less expensive and so forth. Unfortunately, you haven't come down from a mountain and you can't walk on water! But in a trusting working environment, well-established relationships with all relevant stakeholders can still move mountains.

Michael Spandau (SVP for Global IT—Fender Musical Instruments)[4]

During the interview process I would want to get a good understanding the type of CIO the company wants to hire. Is it more infrastructure focused? Or does it include business applications and ERP? It might also include leading the new digital strategy. I'd also like to understand the incentive structure and how that correlates with business outcomes and the goals of the CIO. Ideally there is a very strong correlation. Look for potential pitfalls, such as an in-flight ERP program that is not going well. In summary, you want to be sure that the expectations of the role are well aligned with your personal skill set and experience.

There are certain things I would focus on in the first 90–100 days. First building relationships with the following groups: executives and business leaders, my own staff, external customers and, finally, informal leaders. I would meet with constituents of all groups and have dedicated in-person two-hour-long sessions. These sessions should focus on what is "top of mind" for each group, what keeps them up at night, how do they set their goals and what makes them successful.

The informal leaders are a critical stakeholder group since it can be very telling what they have to offer. You can learn how people make decisions and the culture of the organization. How do they define success? How do they celebrate accomplishments and how do they deal with challenges? Get a general sense of the inner workings of the organization.

Beyond the first 90 days, I would focus on five key activities an IT organization provides: First, keep the lights on. Don't break anything! Make sure the company is able to operate because it will immediately reflect on you if things don't go well. Second, focus on new projects that will generate quick wins. The third item is business intelligence (BI). Every leader has a need for improved BI. I would spend a lot of time understanding the quality and usage of BI. The fourth item is cybersecurity. Make sure that any major cybersecurity gaps are addressed. The fifth item is any external or internal compliance requirements.

Another important area is the budget. Depending on where in the annual budget cycle you join the organization, you might be asked to develop a budget rather quickly. This requires a good understanding of the existing budget, how it was developed and what assumptions were made.

I recommend avoiding making any long-term decisions early on. Every IT supplier will want to meet with you and sell you the latest and greatest. No need to make quick decision and long-term commitments. Don't succumb to this temptation.

Most importantly, don't set expectations too high. Don't promise anything you can't deliver. Sometimes a new leader will try to make changes too fast in order to make a big impression. Resist this temptation.

Eric Saracchi (Chief Information Officer, Firmenich)[5]

I have worked at Firmenich for 27 years. We had three CIO leaders in quick succession, and I was asked if I wanted to take over the role. I had previously led the enterprise-wide ERP program that had been very successful. My boss immediately informed me that I needed to reduce IT spending by 20% which also included headcount reductions. The rationale was that IT spending as a percentage of sales was too high. I was immediately thrust into a turnaround situation. The headcount reductions would also require re-organizing the IT function. I also found out that as soon as you are CIO, executives' laptops are too heavy and battery life is too short. I was getting buried in issues like that!

There was no on-boarding process and I realized that I needed help. I had developed a very good external network and met with the former CIO of a large international consumer products company who offered to coach me through reducing costs and re-organizing the IT function. He also coached me on how to work with the business leaders. Leading the ERP program provided the opportunity to build relationships with "post-sales" business leaders, but I had not worked with the "pre-sales" leaders in product development, sales and so forth. Therefore, even though I was an insider, I had to build a new set of relationships internally. This CIO coach really helped me do that.

I also worked with a leadership coach who helped me develop the leadership skills that the new role required. What makes you a great individual contributor doesn't necessarily make you a good manager. Likewise, what makes you a great manager does not necessarily make you a great leader and I wanted help in that transition. I also engaged someone to help me with design thinking and digital innovation. Just like an athlete works with different coaches, I built a team of advisors to coach me in my transition as CIO. You can achieve great results with coaches, but you need to be open.

You have to engage your team in a different way as CIO. My team was resistant to the changes in organization structure and focus. I changed out my entire first line of management with people who were aligned to the new mission. We also focused on innovation and improving service. It took a lot of sweat and tears to accomplish this realignment over three years. I also fired our biggest IT vendors because they were unwilling to support our cost reduction efforts. We eventually cut 25% out of our IT cost and that freed up 5% to re-invest in new projects.

You have to develop an elevator speech to give to senior executives that is really powerful. A speech about how IT can address business issues. Leading a well-funded ERP program is different because it is so large and risky that the executive committee funds it without constant re-justification. However, as CIO you need to justify every additional investment.

As a new CIO, you need to surround yourself with the right people both internally and externally. You have to work on your team and you have to work on yourself, because what got you promoted will not be sufficient for you to succeed in a new role. You need to build bridges by addressing the main issues of your business partners. You need to be business savvy and prove to others that you can move from being a good manager to a business leader.

Gary Hayes (SVP and CIO, CenterPoint Energy)[6]

One of the greatest, and simplest, advice someone gave me in my consulting years was that clients wanted and needed "confident leadership". The light went on, it was not about "it depends" but it was about providing clarity and a pathway to succeed. Yes, many times that pathway is twisted or turned but you have the confidence to adapt and deliver.

Think of it this way. If you are going to the top of Everest, you want the Sherpa that understands the path, is attuned and responds to dangers and changing nature of the environment. But most importantly, one that gives you the confidence that you are going to make it to the top and come back for the next adventure.

This is your role as the CIO! You must provide that confident leadership that brings clarity to the path, to recognize the dangers and changing natures, to provide the approaches that allows your team (data center to executive leadership) to be successful. At the same time, you are addressing your own set of dangers and changing nature of managing a technology organization in today's fast changing world.

The path is not always successful. You must learn from the missteps along the way, but too many people dwell on those missteps. Recognize what is done is done, align and confidently get back on the path—confident adaptation to lead again. Your team will need this lesson. In the heat of the battle, don't worry how you got there, successfully get out and back to normality! You must define, learn and prevent the issue in the future which is yet another challenge.

Your role is to understand the needs of top managers down to the individuals on your team. You must distill these inputs, since your role puts you in the center of many disparate conversations, and then translate those inputs into a direction, strategy and/or roadmap. You must look constantly over the horizon! Not for all the new, bright and shiny technology objects but for the "solutions" which enable your organization to be successful. I've always considered a "solution" as the nexus where strategy, people, process and technology intertwine to provide value. You are the orchestrator of the solution.

When I became the CIO, I did the 90-day plan and it did help in the transition. But what next? I spent time with the executive leadership team, business partners, my leadership team and employees to rationalize what I had heard and observed. I gathered my career experiences in operations, consulting, technology and life and realized one of the key messages that my team needed to hear was they were equally part of the business. They were just not the "technology order takers". They had a critical role in the success of the company.

I realized we needed clarity to our path forward. The rapid change and adoption of technology in both the information and operational areas of the company was at an ever-accelerating pace while the obligation of strong cost management persists. This "technology paradox" is other key learning. It is true: it is all about execution. Whether that execution is the day-to-day reliable operations, delivering projects or organizational transformation. A key structure I put in place was a "Strategic Execution Office" for the technology organization. It is the project management office (PMO) for our strategy and transformation initiatives. To transform the company and the technology required commitment to a set of accepted outcomes driven by the SEO.

Teams were given outcomes, assignments and required to track and document results. Now a little balance in this, we had constraints on resources, funding and normal operations—but, those were acceptable variations to the schedule but not the targeted results. Our focus was the destination. The key was not to let these efforts become the "flavor of the day" but to make sure we delivered results. This has served us well. It provided clarity to the resources involved, it provided opportunity for new leadership development, and we improved our organizational outcomes. Drive your strategy and roadmap and do not let it become a flavor of the day.

Last thought, I learned a long time ago that there is a "customer at the end of every process". At the end of every technology is a customer or user. It is easy in a technology organization to overlook this. It is easy for the organization to drift away in the hardware, software and cloud and forget that enablement is at the heart of what we do. The customer and user experience is the defining success. This is your measure of success.

The CIO experience is a tremendously challenging and yet rewarding role you will experience in your career. I hope this helps you to look over the horizon and be the confident leader, the Sherpa, that transforms your organization.

Gerry Mecca (Former VP and CIO, Keurig Dr. Pepper)[7]

I think most companies don't know how to hire a CIO. Everyone knows what a good VP-Marketing, CFO or VP-HR looks like in terms of capabilities and experience. Most recruit CIOs based on a set of generic leadership qualities and do not really appreciate how unique the CIO role is in terms of breadth of functional understanding and depth of technology experience. Companies really need to understand the qualities of an IT leader.

Presuming you have already gotten past the recruiter and this is the interview stage with the hiring manager, preferably the CEO, use the five "B's": "be brief baby be brief". You are a CIO and, after all, only you care about how deep or how wide you are. You wouldn't be sitting there if your reputation didn't precede you. There will be the usual set questions you'd better have the straightforward answer to but make sure you flip the script as early as you can and ask "what the biggest problem" you are being asked to solve or "what key goal or objective" has the organization in mind for IT to help achieve. Then listen! Your next few questions should be around deeper understanding of whatever the answer to your fist question would be and then, if the time is right, ask if you can offer some thoughts about how to address those problems or needs. Remember the 5 "B's".

In the first 90 days, get to know the key stakeholders and the current state of IT. Of course, if IT operations is a disaster, get in and get to the bottom of it as you don't get to do anything if the lights are off or flickering. But, as soon as possible, you must hear from the business exactly what is expected of IT from them and how IT has done so far. It is important to ask a lot of follow up questions and don't just accept the first thing they tell you, because they won't tell you the whole story in the beginning. Ask "tell me more" and then be quiet and listen! You also need to be ready to act when someone gives you a problem to solve.

Your next three months should be working the answers into an action plan and a strategy to get to a better place. Quick wins are a must and you must get them done. I define quick wins as things that you can complete in the first 90–100 days to win favor with the executive team. Something that you can fix relatively quickly like service delivery issues or other operational challenges. Most of these opportunities come from your initial discussions with stakeholders. Large-scale change requires a deeper dive and more time to evaluate, but there are usually small things you can fix quickly to give you some momentum.

Get a mentor right away, someone close who you can trust. In one assignment I went to the HR business partner and asked to identify a good mentor who knew the business well. In another organization, I asked the president of one of the business units. I told him I just wanted to have someone who knew the organization that I could bounce ideas off of. He was flattered and agreed and helped me a lot.

You also need to assess your team and decide who the keepers are and who to release. However, don't clean house wholesale unless it's really needed because I've seen CIOs get burned by making rash decisions about people. I like the organization model of having VPs reporting to me who all have a combination of operational, delivery and innovation accountabilities. They are aligned to a part of the business taking IT demand, but can't just throw it over the wall because they are also accountable for operations. They need to view themselves as partnering with the business.

Lastly, transparency in IT governance is essential. Tell the business what you are going to do on an annual basis, report progress quarterly and include your business partners in those decisions. Cover what is happening now, what is proposed in the near future and the financials for the IT organization. Importantly, always provide a roadmap.

Robert J. Webb (Former CIO—MetLife Japan, Etihad Airways, Hilton Hotels, Equifax Global, GE)[8]

I am a student and practitioner of large-scale change. On the surface, change happens very quickly, but deep change of the type involved with digital transformation or leveraging information technology for growth, productivity and profitability occurs much more slowly than most of us imagine or would like. Expectations for the pace of change are typically not well set.

I would advise any incoming CIO to meet with as many people as possible such as the board of directors, C-level executives and leaders lower in the organization so you can really understand the culture, the people and the existing situation. It is especially important to understand the use of information technology, the role of the CIO and the history that exists in the company. I recommend that CIOs look at five key areas: culture, people, technology infrastructure, finances and partnerships.

Culture can be assessed by asking about past "traumas" and how they were dealt with. For example, an ERP project that was way over budget, a failed vendor relationship or a key person who left the company. How did the organization respond? Were lessons learned and applied? What is the accountability framework for realizing business benefits from information technology investments? People means looking at the organization chart. What are the structural relationships in the organization? What are the roles? What are the staffing levels? What is the proportion of resources that are insourced versus outsourced. The technology infrastructure is straightforward: reviewing the technical footprint, applications inventory and current projects. It's also important to look for redundancies because many times several versions of an application may have emerged in an organization. Finances is looking at the annual reports and 10Ks for a public company, understanding the cash flows, the OPEX and CAPEX budgets and revenue projections. Partnerships refer to the strength of the relationships within the company, for example, how tight is the top management team. You can map this out using a genogram style chart with lines, colors and symbols of how you rate the strength of relationships. Don't forget to look lower in the organization such as the executive teams' direct reports. The other aspect of partnerships is reviewing agreements with external partners such as software providers. You want to understand the strength of the relationship as well as the strength of the contracts. How are communications patterns and where have they broken down in the past?

One question I ask is: "is there any risk that I need to know about that might put us on the front page of the *Wall Street Journal*?" You can get interesting answers that range from "I don't know" to very specific issues around, for example, security and privacy.

I think that Michael Watkins' book *The First 90 Days* is a great resource at the beginning. I had the opportunity to attend a two-day workshop with him at IMD Business School in Lausanne. However, I don't agree with the advice to get quick wins or "putting points on the board". While it might be a popular notion, I think it comes from a feeling of inferiority on the part of the CIO, that the new CIO must prove himself/herself by delivering something fast. I've seen a lot of people step into roles and try to make change quickly and the organization rejects it. First you have to understand the issue fully and realize that changing the organization will take longer than you expect. If you focus on quick wins you can create unrealistic expectations and it puts pressure on the organization that isn't sustainable.

You need to emphasize to your Board and management team that this is a three- to five-year journey. You may need to educate the Board and suggest creating a technology subcommittee if one doesn't already exist. Computing is evolving and retiring legacy applications in large organizations takes time. You're really rebuilding the house brick by brick. Digital transformation is driving more decentralized responsibility for digital innovation and this is a big cultural shift in most organizations. You need to balance this trend with more centralized control over areas such as security and infrastructure reliability.

I just finished research into successful digital transformations and found that there were three common success factors. They were enhanced CIO listening skills, greater customer orientation and low CIO ego, that is, the CIO co-develops solutions rather than driving solutions solely from the IT organization. These are all soft skills and have nothing to do with information technology!

Lastly, the CIO has more opportunity to make an impact on financials than they normally think. Rationalizing the applications portfolio can yield dramatic decreases in operating expense. Negotiations with suppliers can also reduce expenses significantly. Finance is the language of the business. You need to be able to articulate what it costs to run the IT portfolio and what the investment plan looks like. After about six months, you should be able to communicate the roadmap to the Board and executive team.

John Lawson (CIO—BAE Systems PLC)[9]

As well as the basics of research, research, research, during the interview stage, I would advise any potential new CIO to form a viewpoint on how the new world digital economy factors will shape the company in the coming years and a vision for how the new CIO will help to shape and drive the digital agenda. Whether or not the CIO is directly responsible for the digital agenda or works in support of a chief digital officer (CDO), this viewpoint is critical. It's worthwhile having a wide view on this and exploring how other organizations—both peers and competitors—are pushing the boundaries to become dominant in their respective industries, via the digital agenda. Digital technical architectural skills are essential of course, but so is an awareness of other factors such as the role that digital people/culture, the potential for competitor collaboration, the potential for new business models. Both internal operations and product/service offerings should also be considered.

Go into the first 100 days knowing that in 100 days, you will be asked to present your observations plus your strategic direction and plans. Create an outline or storyboard of the presentation as early as possible and use the next 100 days to populate it with facts, details and visions for the future. A critical area of learning is the language of the company, that is, specific terminology, acronyms, phrases and concepts that resonate with the stakeholders. Some of them will be widely used already, some not—but don't be ashamed to copy shamelessly and utilize what has been done previously when it makes sense, when it fits with your personal style, agenda and vision.

During the first 100 days you should be spending limited time in your own office. It is critical to get out around the business. Spend time with your own team but equally, spending time with stakeholders within the business and your suppliers will be crucial. Your approach for the many meetings you will be having needs to form into a repeatable process to understand each of the stakeholder domains, understand existing projects, form a view on the vision and build relationships. Having a standard set of (simple) questions and a standard format to capture your notes will help. It will also help to capture your thoughts on if the person(s) you are meeting with are supporters or detractors of IT; this will be useful as you create a stakeholder communications plan designed to build your relationships over the longer term.

You should fully understand any major in-flight projects. Assess these projects as you would have done with successful projects from your past. If you spot any deficiencies in how the projects are being run or any missing components, highlight the issues and address them. You will have the benefit of an outside point of view only for a limited time and you should capitalize on this. Ultimately, you should be looking for specific opportunities to make a "step change" in the business value that IT can deliver for the organization. This may come from specific digital initiatives that deliver value in a standalone capacity or from a portfolio of existing projects plus new ones that you may instigate to help articulate a roadmap of change and improved business value.

Don't underestimate the value of solid, rigorous governance processes. Again, as the new person in the team you can help inject new energy and a new approach (if needed)—understand the key business risks (with regard to IT) and make sure you are giving them significant air time in the right discussions (especially cyber security). Meet with your critical suppliers. Understand the situation from their side. Some will continue to be essentially, others less so, but make sure they know your role and what you are there to do.

Look for opportunities to present your 100-day observations and strategy to as many senior stakeholder groups as possible, ultimately to the Executive Committee (EC) and Board. Ensure that your CEO and other senior EC members fully understand that you are not in your role to keep the IT lights on and that your ambition is to be a key part of their team driving both operational excellence and significant business growth.

Richard Corbridge (Director of Innovation, Boots [UK], Former CIO NHS Leeds Teaching Hospitals Trust, CIO Health Service Executive in Ireland and CEO eHealth Ireland, and CIO National Institute for Health Research)[10]

New anything unnerves the best of us, each time you become the new CIO, it is a giant leap into the unknown, no matter the experiences you have or the capability you demonstrated in your last role, the next role will always be different and initially harder than you remember!

Why? Because the CIO role is now about leading people, and people create cultures, and your CIO leadership will only be successful if you can make the culture work for you in some way. Accepting change and an ability to engage will be the key skill you will need on day one. I remember going to my first all-staff meeting as the first CIO of the Republic of Ireland's health system. I had "stolen" an idea from Frank Buytendijk, the celebrated Gartner analyst, and asked the team to self-nominate whether they were digital evangelists, skeptics or pragmatists? By the end of the session, there was one evangelist, me, the new CIO. The Irish role was the best CIO role I have ever done but I misread the opening environment. The new digital team needed to go on the journey with me, I was a new face, a new voice (with an English accent) and that wasn't going to get me there on day one no matter what enthusiasm I brought to the stage.

Those early days in the role are the moments when you are immersed at the fire hose of new: you have a torrent of new information coming at you at speed, so quickly translating the signal from the noise is the key challenge. This is not just about being able to truly hear the sounds being made but to assess the most important ones as quickly as possible and with a style that will engage the whole team in the journey you are about to embark on together.

My first big CIO role at the clinical research function of the UK's NHS was an exciting new role; however, the fire hose moment was not allowed to last very long, I had to "drink" quickly. I was introduced to the team as the new CIO by the CEO and a few days later we started to insource the outsourced team. At least here we all went through the same change cycle together and at speed, no slow unwrapping of the direction, this was rapid change. It cost us as an organization though, as several organizational structure missteps took valuable time to correct over the ensuing 18 months all of which could have been avoided if just a bit more of time had been spent understanding the two key pillars of the business: the need and the people.

The first days of a new year are referred to by "social scientists" as the temporal landmark. New roles are quite clearly comparable to these landmarks with very specific application to the job we do and the work we love. As humans, we rely on landmarks to navigate geographies, we also need these same marks to navigate time, moments in time that we can come back to, moments in time that will allow and enable us to reflect and learn. Dan Pink in *When* discusses these temporal landmarks as the opening of "new mental accounts" the ability to start a new fiscal year with a nice white set of ledger columns! I have yet to meet a CIO who has been allowed to do this.

While it is so important to create your own new account, it is essential for success to understand the balance sheet left for you, the profit and loss that had been made and try to learn from that. The biggest mistake a new CIO can make is to "rub out" or alter the previous accounts. The first 100 days are going to be hard enough, so land softly and make the most of what went before, making gentle in roads in a collaborative way that takes the team on the journey with you and allows them to inform your direction. You may know how to be a CIO, but a generic CIO will not work "here" you need to be the CIO of the organization not just "a" CIO.

Matthew Syed in *Rebel Ideas* provides insight into why he, along with Manoj Badale (a technology leader), Sue Campbell (an administrator of the Olympics), Sir Michael Barber (an educationalist), Stuart Lancaster (Head coach of the England Rugby team), Sir David Brailsford (a cycling coach) and Lucy Giles (college commander of the Royal Sandhurst Academy) were asked to be the advisory board of the England Football team when Gareth Southgate took over as manager. The media had a field day when this happened, why did the Football Association (FA) ask experts in Rugby, Cycling and table tennis to advise on why the England team was so hapless when it came to large tournaments. Syed points out though that seeking advice from the same people who KNOW FOOTBALL wouldn't change anything, Southgate wanted to hear something new. This is something I tried hard as I became the CIO in Ireland, I gave myself as much opportunity to meet people from throughout the technology ecosystem in Ireland as I did the specific healthcare teams. This gave me a chance to understand the national culture, people and business need with a new lens, which I think contributed to the success that was made of the first CIO role in Ireland and the office that came with it.

When I became the CIO in the NHS in Leeds, I quickly learned that the language across the healthcare system had become corrupt over time. What the clinical teams wanted, needed and had was very different to what the organization thought they had, could afford and, indeed strategically, were willing to shoot for. The CIO in a new role needs to learn quickly to translate the business languages, and to use that language knowledge as a ventriloquist throughout the team (yes, I did say ventriloquist!). The CIO now needs the team to talk the same language that they do, not the language that they have always spoken.

When I started to create a vision and purpose for the digital team in the Leeds NHS, I used a method known as Very Clear Ideas[11] to create engagement and buy in on where we should go. Using this process, I asked a wide representation of the team to come together to create a representation of our vision, our purpose and even to review the initial governance and leadership structures. In that group was every type of person and role from across the team and they created every artifact that would be needed to lead digital across the business, and funnily enough, the team got behind the way forward.

A new CIO role is full of excitement. Enjoy the sleepless nights of the new role, with your mind buzzing with new ideas. Remember, your job is to help everyone make sense of what digital can do for them and then to help them all collaborate to be the best they can be at the business they are in. In three years, if you are still the CIO, try to make yourself go through this cycle again to ensure what you are doing is still relevant, fresh and that the maximum the business can get from you is being delivered. Most of all, enjoy the ride.

Notes

1. K. Alber. Phone interview by Tony Gerth, August 12, 2019.
2. Dr. M. Müller-Wünsch. Personal interview by Joe Peppard, November 11, 2019.
3. In Germany, company law, the *Aktiengesetz*, requires all public companies (*Aktiengesellschaften*) to have two boards: a management board called a *Vorstand* and a supervisory board called an *Aufsichtsrat*. The supervisory board, is essentially the board of directors and oversees and appoints the members of the management board and must approve major business decisions.
4. M. Spandau. Phone interview by Tony Gerth, August 27, 2019.
5. E. Saracchi. Phone interview by Tony Gerth, October 8, 2019.
6. G. Hayes. Written response to Tony Gerth, October 21, 2019.
7. G. Mecca. Phone interview by Tony Gerth, October 29, 2019.
8. R. Webb. Phone interview by Tony Gerth, October 28, 2019.
9. J. Lawson. Written response to Tony Gerth, October 22, 2019.
10. R. Corbridge. Written response to Joe Peppard, October 30, 2019.
11. Very Clear Ideas—https://www.howtobeclear.com/cards

Index[1]

---

[1] Note: Page numbers followed by 'n' refer to notes.

Printed by Printforce, the Netherlands